Salt Water
Fly Fishing

Salt Water Fly Fishing

Joe Brooks

With a new Foreword by Joe Healy,
Editor of *Salt Water Fly Fishing* magazine

THE DERRYDALE PRESS

LANHAM AND NEW YORK

THE DERRYDALE PRESS

Published in the United States of America
by The Derrydale Press
4720 Boston Way, Lanham, Maryland 20706

Distributed by NATIONAL BOOK NETWORK, INC.

New foreword copyright © 2000 BY JOE HEALY
First Derrydale paperback printing with french folds 2000

Library of Congress Cataloging-in-Publication Data

Brooks, Joe, 1905–1972.
    Salt water fly fishing / Joe Brooks.
        p. cm.
    Originally published: New York : Putnam, 1950. With a new foreword.
    ISBN 1-58667-007-7 (pbk. : alk. paper)
    1. Saltwater fishing. 2. Fly casting. I. Title.

SH457.B7 2000
799.1'6—DC21   00-025870

TO MARY

THE NAMES used for the various fishes with which this book deals are in accordance with the *Standard Check List of Common Names for Principal American Sport Fishes*, as compiled by the Outdoor Writers Association of America.

Contents

Contents

Illustrations

Foreword

THE text of the book that's now in your hands was first published in 1950 by G. P. Putnam's Sons, New York. It has been a definitive resource, right from the start. Books predating this one may have touched on anglers casting flies in salt water (as indeed they were before the twentieth century) or listed fly patterns for saltwater duty, but as the title tells us, *Salt Water Fly Fishing* was the first book to train a focus solely on the sport.

Even though this new edition from Derrydale Press marks the book's golden anniversary, we can't assess the value of the book only by its age. So much of Joe Brooks' writing remains useful today that if this were the first printing, the angling world would have to consider it a vital text. My hunch will be proved true if it's your first time reading the book.

I've read *Salt Water Fly Fishing* a half-dozen times, and I'm still astounded by how instructive the book is; I'm also struck by how entertaining and crisp Brooks' prose is. I've learned much from the book, as legions of anglers have.

Foreword

I first discovered *Salt Water Fly Fishing* right about the time I was discovering saltwater fly fishing. It was the early 1990s and I was living in New York and working as a staff editor at *Outdoor Life*, for which magazine Brooks was a frequent contributor in the 1950s and served as fishing editor from 1968 to 1972. The library at the magazine's office was filled with various editions of out-of-print books, many of which were written by former and current contributors to the magazine, and amid the stacks I found a weathered first edition of this book. I read every page that afternoon. What did I learn? That bonefish prefer to feed into a current, that tarpon will hit fly-rod poppers, and that by watching gulls working bait I could follow the movements of schools of striped bass. That's what I remember now. Who knows how much I've retained latently as foundation for what I know about the sport, and what I continue to learn?

A Maryland native, Brooks himself was introduced to saltwater fly fishing in the 1920s by fly-tying innovator Tom Loving when the two fished for shad, striped bass, and brackish-water largemouth bass in the Susquehanna River and other tributaries of Chesapeake Bay. Brooks often wrote of his fly-fishing experiences in the pages of *Outdoor Life*, but it was this book that gave generations of anglers an instruction manual on casting flies in the brine. Indeed, the publication of the book in 1950 not only legitimized the sport of saltwater fly fishing as a discipline unto itself, but also exposed gung-ho sportsmen in post-war America to an entirely new concept in fishing and catching large, speedy ocean fish with fly tackle. The author of this book deserves much of the credit for introducing saltwater fly fishing to a mass audience.

It was no coincidence that soon after the book was published a national movement began to evolve whose aim was to collectively build their experiential know-how of saltwater fly fishing tactics, ocean fish, and coastal fisheries. Later on, in the 1960s, Joe Brooks helped found The Salt Water Fly Rodders of America, a national group that brought together anglers who had an affinity for casting flies for saltwater species.

Brooks continued his saltwater fishing throughout the 1950s, 60s, and 70s, catching such fish as the first recorded permit on fly tackle; a 148-pound tarpon that for some time was a fly-rod world record; and in 1957, a 19-pound, 8-ounce permit in Cuba that still stands as an International Game Fish Association tippet-class world record. Before he became known for fly fishing, Brooks was an all-star athlete and a semi-pro football player, a member of the Baltimore Orioles farm team, and a sparring partner to Jack Dempsey. Brooks died in 1972, and is buried in Livingston, Montana.

Many of today's best-known saltwater fly fishers were influenced or mentored by Joe Brooks. Lefty Kreh, the sport's current leading man, was a close friend of Brooks for several decades. After helping Lefty pick out his first fly outfit in the late 1940s, a South Bend fiberglass rod and GAF line, Brooks gave Lefty his first fly-casting lesson. "Joe was one of the greatest people to get involved with fly fishing," Lefty says. "He introduced legions of people to fishing, especially other writers." Lefty says that one of Brooks' greatest contributions to the sport was opening up new fly-fishing destinations, such as Canada, New Zealand, south Florida and the Florida Keys.

Fly-tackle-developer Cam Sigler calls Brooks "Gentleman Joe, truly a gentleman." Cam met Brooks in 1957; today Cam says that Brooks influenced not only his choice of career, but his entire life. "The things he taught were honesty and integrity, in whatever you do." Chico Fernandez met Brooks at the Miami Beach Rod & Reel Club in the 1950s and calls him "a mentor and teacher."

Tarpon guru Stu Apte has said that Brooks was a second father to him. Indeed, when I visited Stu at his home in the Florida Keys, he wore a look of reverence when he took down from his bookshelf a first edition of this book signed to him by the author. Stu also played a tape of an episode of *Wide World of Sports* from the 1960s during which he guided Joe Brooks for tarpon in the Florida Keys.

Joe Brooks did more than anyone to popularize the sport of saltwater fly fishing, and with popularity came the advancements in techniques and the refinements in tackle from which we profit today.

On the way through this book, Brooks may provoke you to rethink some of today's conventions on the sport. A good example comes in the chapter simply entitled "Equipment." Here, Brooks states that a slow-action 9 1/2-foot fly rod is best for saltwater fishing. His reasons? "The bigger, slower rod allows you to shoot the line greater distances with less effort." Nowadays, fast, stiff fly rods are most common for saltwater fishing, though bit by bit anglers seem to be rediscovering the attributes of slower-action rods.

Of course, at the time Brooks was writing the book, he was using 9-1/2-foot bamboo rods with nylon GAF or torpedo-head fly lines. Still, half a century after he committed his thoughts to paper, his advice on choosing a fly rod bears our consideration. Put another way, although the fly tackle we use in saltwater today has changed considerably from what anglers used in the 1950s, Brooks' common-sense view of how to use the stuff still stands.

Okay, enough of the then-versus-now comparison. Let's talk about this book's value as a cultural artifact. Simply put, it's a historical treasure. Brooks gives ample credit to the pioneers who were proving that saltwater fish could be taken with fly tackle back in the early and mid part of the twentieth century—anglers such as Tom Loving, Holmes Allen, Allen Corson, among others—and he produces a living record to the memory of anglers such as Jimmie Albright, Red Greb, Harold Gibbs, Harry Snow, and Herb Welsh, men whose names are still spoken in fly-fishing circles.

A friend of mine, Vin Sparano, former editor in chief of *Outdoor Life* and an editor at the magazine when Brooks was the fishing editor, told me that Brooks "was a guy without a hint of ego." You'll have that same opinion as you encounter Brooks' anecdotes about early saltwater fly fishing. He always gives credit to those who lent a helping hand in his discoveries about the sport. In the chapter "Bonefish," in particular,

Brooks cites the many teachers from whom his salt-water fly-fishing education came.

Right now, I'm looking out on the oceanside flats of Islamorada in the Florida Keys, one of the areas about which Brooks writes in these pages. He fished here in the late 1940s with Jimmie and Frankee Albright, and by his own count had caught some 250 bonefish at the time *Salt Water Fly Fishing* was first published. I'm thinking about how it must have been 50 years ago: almost no development along U.S. 1, few boats on the water and certainly no jet skis, vast schools of unpressured bonefish darkening the crystal blue waters as they push into the current, excavating the sandy bottom for crabs, shrimp, and small baitfish.

It's time for me to take a cue from Brooks, string up my progressive-action graphite fly rod with my specialty saltwater fly line, and head out to enjoy, as Brooks called it, "the world's most satisfactory sport." I think today I'll try casting an Upperman Joe Brooks Bucktail. (For the recipe, see page 34.)

Joe Healy, Editor
Saltwater Fly Fishing magazine
Islamorada, Florida
February, 2000

Introduction

THE history of salt-water fishing with a fly rod goes back a long way. There is a record of an angler taking shad on a fly on the Susquehanna River in Maryland seventy-five years ago. Twenty-seven years ago, Tom Loving of Baltimore, who introduced me to salt-water fly-fishing, was catching stripers up to twenty-five pounds on large white bucktails. At about the same time, Tom turned out the first fly tied especially for shad, and pioneered the brackish-water largemouth bass.

Some of the old-timers also fished the shallow flats off the Florida coast for many species of fish that will strike at a fly. Howard Bonbright caught tarpon with a fly of his own fashioning down there, many years ago. H. J. Greb, seventy-year-old Miami man, tied feathery foolers for snook, tarpon, and many other salt-water game fish and followed up with some of the earliest bonefish flies.

Throughout the years a few such lone sportsmen, here and there, have been taking salt-water fish with flies of their own design. Other anglers heard about these pioneers and were aware that they were catching plenty of nice fish. It remains a mystery why more of them did not take advantage of this tremendous field of sport fishing. Only during the past few years have the masses of anglers, who used to stow their fishing equipment away with the coming of the first snow, begun to realize that in the southern salt are dozens of potential light-tackle game fish, and that northern coastal waters abound with similar opportunities throughout most of the year.

The Susquehanna, the Chickahominy River near Richmond, Virginia, the Connecticut, and the Potomac have become well-known shad-fishing rivers. Many other streams which shad ascend to spawn, from northern Florida to the St. Lawrence watershed, will produce fly-fishing—provided, of course, that the water is clear, that it is shallow where you fish, and that there is a current. Shad are also found on the Pacific Coast where anglers at many scattered points in Oregon and California are discovering that they will take a fly.

The brackish-water largemouth black bass, so well known in North Carolina, Georgia, Florida, Delaware, Maryland, Virginia, and other coastal waters, is now a favorite with thousands of fly rodders. The readiness of brackish-water largemouth black bass to strike a streamer fly or a surface popping bug has made this species very popular with the light-tackle fraternity.

Another coastal favorite, the striped bass, is sensational as he swirls under and finally, when your heart is in your mouth, takes a popping bug or a big white bucktail. Twenty-pound stripers are not unusual on fly tackle, while four- and five-pound fish are an everyday affair. Stripers have wide distribution on the Atlantic Coast, ranging from Florida to the Gulf of St. Lawrence; since being introduced on the Pacific Coast in 1896, they have extended their range from Monterey, California, to and beyond the Umpqua River in Oregon.

While fly-fishing in Pacific salty waters is really new, it is rapidly taking hold, and California, Oregon, and Washington anglers have discovered that the silver salmon and the chinook or king salmon will take a fly now and again, if a little temperamentally, while the California sea bass, which hang around rocks and jetties, will strike either a popping bug or a bucktail and put up a swell fight.

Spotted sea trout (weakfish) are suckers for a popping bug. They also slap a streamer hard and like a spinner-bucktail or a spinner-streamer combination. They range from New York down the Atlantic Coast, throughout the middle Atlantic states to Florida, and around and off the Gulf States.

In Florida, a whole new crop of fish is providing grand angling for a growing army of fly rodders. The shallows off the southern coast of that state are teeming with many varieties of fish which will hit a fly. Tarpon, snook, snappers, jack, barracuda, bonefish, ladyfish, channel bass, spotted sea trout, and many other salt-water gamesters are avid takers of artificial fly-rod lures.

Even before the shallows of the Florida coast had attracted many light-tackle enthusiasts, however, a most interesting development had occurred along the now-famous Tamiami Trail. This highway was built in 1926 and 1927, and as the trail progressed westward from Miami, water filled in the ditches which had been dredged out to provide the roadbed. It wasn't long before adventurous Miami bass fishermen were working these new roadside "canals." Bob Aiken, Captain Stewart Miller,

Introduction

Milton Drenner, and Holmes Allen blazed that trail using the Wilder-Dilg wounded minnow as a lure. Bass were everywhere and it was fishing to write home about. They followed the work crew westward, tossing their lures into ever new water and having the time of their lives. Then, seventeen miles out from Miami, things really happened. Lateral canals from the Gulf of Florida joined the canals along the Trail, and salt mingled with the canal waters on both sides of the road. Along with the salt came salt-water fish—baby tarpon and snook. The anglers started using bucktails and then streamers, flairing the feathers by reversing them. Those four Miamians were right on the spot, hitting that virgin fishing bang on the nose. It must have been wonderful.

After these first Trail fishermen came many other anglers. Fishing was so good that Homer Rhode, Jr., who tied some of the first flies especially designed for those new canal denizens, reported strikes on almost every cast.

While this book is concerned only with fly-fishing, I feel that great credit should be extended to the many plug casters who played a large part in starting the light-tackle fishing in Florida waters. Bill Ackerman, well-known outdoor writer, was one of those fine tackle advocates and did much to further that type of sporty fishing, and many an enthusiastic fly rodder has followed trails blazed by Bill.

Allen Corson was probably the first one to catch sea trout on plugs in New Jersey waters. He brought years of such light-tackle salt-water experience along when he moved to Miami, where he is now fishing editor of the *Miami Herald.* Corson has done a bang-up job for anglers in Southern Florida. He has plugged light-tackle fishing in his column and has at all times kept up to the latest in angling methods. He went for salt-water fly-fishing in a big way and talked and wrote about it at every opportunity. He has made a study of the tackle needed and, finding the proper equipment, has advised hundreds of fly casters on the right setup for willow-wanding salt water. His contribution has helped as much as anyone's to build up the present-day popularity of salt-water light-tackle fishing.

Needless to say, all the pioneering has not yet been done, and every season sees new species added to the list of those which have been captivated by a flirting fly. One of the most interesting of these additions was a 41-pound lemon shark landed in the winter of 1949 by Jack Ardis, Miami Beach sportsman. In early May, 1950, while fishing Content Key with Captain Leo Johnson of Islamorada, Florida, I took a 5-pound 10-ounce permit and also two species of grunt—the black and the yellow. None of these fish had formerly been recorded by a fly rodder.

Nor are fly rods confined to the shallow waters. Many fish that swim the reefs can be coaxed up to a fly, and some of the Gulf Stream fish will fall for a well-presented streamer. One afternoon in 1948, Lee Cuddy of Miami took sixteen dolphin, up to ten pounds, while casting a streamer in the Gulf Stream; and in 1949, while I was Manager of the Metropolitan Miami Fishing Tournament, three young lads from Miami reported to me that on a trip to Bimini they had landed a 14½-pound dolphin on fly rod, as well as half a dozen others which were only slightly smaller. And there are many other potential fly takers in the Gulf Stream.

Similarly, while visiting Bermuda in the summer of 1949, I took ten varieties of fish, most of which had not been regarded as susceptible to flies. These included the horse-eye jack, *caranx latus*, the madregal or Bermuda bonito, *seriola falcatus*, the crevalle, *caranx guara*, the gaff topsail pompano, *trachinotus palometo*, the yellowtail, *ocyurus chrysurus*, the Bermuda chub, *kyphosus sectatrix*, the gray snapper, *lutianus griseus*, barracuda, *sphyraena barracuda*, the glasseye, *priacanthus avenatus*, and the mackerel, *euthynnus alleteratus*.

However, the taking of such fish, from the Gulf Stream and from the deeper waters around Bermuda, represents a more exotic phase of the sport of fly-fishing the salt. And while these branches of the game are covered in the following chapters, the bulk of this book is devoted to the more accessible angling along United States coastal waters.

My own first adventure into the salt came after twenty-five years of fly-rod fishing in the conventional, time-honored manner. I was a dry-fly fisherman from away back, brought up on eastern brown trout streams and imbued with all the lore of the purest of the purists. Then Tom Loving took me out after shad, stripers, and brackish-water largemouth bass. We used big bucktails for the stripers, smaller ones for the shad, and large streamers and popping bugs for the bass. We fished mostly around Maryland, in the Susquehanna River below the Conowingo Dam, and in other Chesapeake Bay tributaries—the Severn, the Bush and Middle Rivers, the Gunpowder, and many others. We had rare sport, and as word got around other anglers began to take a more active interest.

After those first salt-water sallies, my fly-rod fishing was not limited to streams and lakes, nor was it limited by season. In the subsequent years I have fished both coasts, from Newfoundland to Florida, and from Alaska to California, and have taken forty-nine species of salt-water fish on a fly at every season of the year. In September, 1948, I landed a striped bass which, as far as is known, is the largest striper ever taken on a fly rod. It came from the waters of Coos Bay, Oregon, and weighed 29 pounds, 6 ounces. In November of 1949, I captured an 11-pound, 5½-ounce bonefish on a fly, at Islamorada, Florida—a record only recently topped by Herb Welsh, famous Maine fly caster, who landed a 12-pound, 4-ounce bonefish while fly-fishing at Islamorada. Between these two widely separated points, I have fished for almost every swimmer of the coastal waters.

This is not written boastfully, but merely to show fly-rod anglers who have not tried the salt that there is a vast field for them to explore. It is a field abundant with great fighting fish, and the purpose of this book is to pass on to other devotees of the fly rod some of my own enthusiasm for what is, to me, the world's most satisfactory sport.

I want to take this opportunity to thank the many guides who have willingly given me the knowledge and ideas of their many years of observing salt-water game fish. Guiding fly-fishermen is hard work and only a great love of the game keeps them going. It has been a pleasure to me to know these men and to fish with them. They have contributed largely to this book.

Introduction

I also want to thank the men who took the pictures shown in the book: Charlie Ebbets, chief photographer of the *Miami News Bureau,* a great photographer in any league and a fine fly caster, and Pete Perinchief and Wilfred Higgs of the *Bermuda News Bureau,* fine picture takers and companions of fly-fishing trips in their country.

J.W.B., JR.

Salt Water
Fly Fishing

1.

Equipment

RODS

Every fly-rod fisherman knows that there is no all-purpose rod—that is, a fly rod that will do for brook trout in a small mountain stream or for Atlantic salmon in the broad reaches of a Canadian river, for bass bug fishing in New York State or for the fast-water steelhead of the Pacific Coast. A man who is going after all these fish must necessarily load himself down until he looks a little like a porcupine, with rod cases sticking out at all angles. But this is not the case in salt-water fly-fishing. In a number of years of experience fishing the salt from the coast of Newfoundland to the tip of Florida and from Alaska to California, and including Bermuda, I have found that there is a single rod which will do the job for me wherever I go and whatever fish I am after. The beauty of this rod is that it can be used for practically every salt-water fish that hits a fly or bug. It does for bonefish, tarpon, barracuda, sea trout, ladyfish, striped bass, channel bass, shad, bluefish, and many other salty gamesters.

The stick which I have found so universally suitable is a 2-piece, 9½-foot rod weighing anywhere from 6¼ to 6¾ ounces. My own favorite Orvis rod weighs 6⅝ ounces. It is

3

a slow or wet fly rod, with the action coming well down into the grip. While there is nothing wrong with a 3-piece rod which meets the other specifications, I advocate the 2-piece because I believe it has more strength and slightly better action.

Often when I have recommended this rod, I have aroused a storm of protest from old fly fishermen. "The rod will be too heavy," and "You'll wear your arm out," are the usual cries.

But such arguments come mainly from those who have beaten themselves down trying to cast a *light* rod under salt-water fishing conditions. The rod advocated above is designed to meet these special conditions and many a time I have taken an unbeliever protestingly out with the 9½-foot rod and brought him back a convert.

The bigger, slow-action rod allows you to shoot the line greater distances with less effort. Its adaptability is amazing. With it you can make short, accurate casts as well as long, difficult ones into the wind. It has power and yet retains the fineness needed for hitting the target on the nose.

The main, and perhaps the most important reason for the slow-action rod is the fact that the lures used in salt-water fly-fishing are large, wind-resistant streamers and popping bugs. The rod must be capable, through its action, of waiting for the slow lure to make its way back and perform a loop before starting on the forward journey. With a stiff, fast, or dry fly action rod, it would be almost impossible to throw such a lure any distance at all.

One of the outstanding advantages of this rod is its ability to perform lengthy casts without excessive false casting. You can pick up 30 feet of line, make your back-

4

cast, and shoot 30 feet. This enables you to present the fly to an oncoming fish when he is 60 feet away. At that distance he is still unable to see you and there is less chance of his seeing the rod than if you are making false casts with which to get the line out. Incidentally, a trick to get a longer throw under the same conditions is to shoot the backcast and thus produce a quicker, longer toss. It's true that you often hook salt-water fish such as the bonefish within 20 or 30 feet, but more often these fish follow the lure for many feet before they take. Hence a 20- or 30-foot cast, followed by a fish, will bring him in so close that he will see you and flush—and for just such a procedure as that, the slower, more powerful rod is needed.

The longer rod helps on the pickup, too, and enables you to get a good, high backcast, which is perhaps the most important part of the casting technique. A good backcast usually means a good forward cast. A sloppy backcast that hits the water in back of you, throws off the whole of your timing, results in poor presentation, and is likely to scare off the quarry altogether. The height of the rod is of further value in imparting action to the lure and thus inviting more strikes. It will also pay off when you are casting into shallow water of 6- or 8-inch depth, in which plenty of fish are caught. It allows you to drop the lure lightly to avoid frightening the fish—and contrary to general opinion, salt-water fish do scare easily at times. The long rod also helps to keep the lure from catching on underwater growths or from fouling on the bottom. With the rod held high it is surprising in what shallow water you can work the fly and catch fish.

There is usually a wind of some degree blowing when an

angler is fishing the great expanse of salt water, and very seldom do you get in a position where you are sheltered from it. But with the 9½-foot, slow-action rod, you can reach out even in a fairly stiff breeze.

It is possible, of course, to take salt-water fish with a 3-, 4- or 5-ounce rod, provided that you have a reel big enough to carry a lot of backing, and one with a dependable drag. Then you can point the tip of the rod in the general direction of the fighting fish and play him off the reel. But the smaller stick must have a matching line and with a line matched to such a light rod you would have a tough time trying to cast a big lure.

With such equipment you could quite conceivably cast downwind, though with no degree of accuracy. But what if a fish is passing upwind of you? That's the time you would wish for a stouter rod—and with the larger stick, in the course of a year, you would have accounted for many fish which otherwise would have got by.

A salt-water fly rod comes in for a lot of abuse. It is used on big, tough fish and must stand long periods of continuous strain when such fish are hooked. All too often, too, the angler picks up too much line and heaves it time and again into the wind. Frequently the line is water-soaked and heavy, thus putting an additional load on the rod tip. Yet unless the rod has been neglected and water allowed to seep under the ferrules, these rods seldom break. It always astonishes me to see how well a fly rod stands up under the brutal beating it gets in ocean fishing.

Only during the past couple of years have manufacturers begun to make a true salt-water fly rod. Heretofore, the sticks used in salt water were salmon, bass bug, steelhead, or any of the larger rods designed for fishing fresh-water lakes and streams. Now, with the tremendous swing to the salt, the manufacturers are speeding production of rods expressly made for this newly popular type of fishing. They are putting on salt-resisting ferrules, guides, and reel seats, and I know of at least one company that has done extensive research on the effects of salt water on the cane, to the extent of forwarding me three sticks to immerse in salt water for a month, to check these effects.

Most of the rods, to date, have been made of cane. There has also been a sprinkling of steel and lately the woven glass rods are beginning to appear in large numbers on the market. While their value has not yet been proved, with the strides made in the last couple of years it looks as if it will not be too long before a very fine rod has been perfected.

My personal preference for the Orvis 9½-foot, 2-piece rod is founded on two years of extensive use. Besides having the proper action, it is impregnated to withstand the salt, sun, and other elements encountered in ocean fishing.

On a recent trip to the Florida Keys I landed a 38-pound tarpon with my Orvis. I fought the silver king hard, laying back on the rod for the entire forty-two minutes it took to boat the fish. I held the rod straight up, my hands steadying it against my chest. That is, it started straight up, but just beyond the ferrule it went out like a continuation of the casting line, following it here and there after the fish. It took a terrific beating but came back as straight as a die. It was a remarkable performance and since that time I have marveled many more times at the ability of these rods to give continuous, better-than-perfect service.

Orvis rods are made at Manchester, Vermont, and their Battenkill 9½-foot, 6⅝-ounce, 2-piece, slow-action rod, with two tips, sells for $82.50. The 2-piece 9½-foot Manchester, made by the same company, lists at $65, has the same slow action, and is a peach of a rod.

The South Bend 2-piece # 51 has also proved to be a good salt-water fly rod. It is 9 feet long and weighs 6 ounces, and is stainless steel equipped. Although a trifle on the fast side as far as action is concerned, a GAF line matches it up well enough to bring out the rod and give a creditable performance. It sells for $25.

Another powerful 2-piece rod is the Winston, made in San Francisco. Due to the hollow bottom section, this fine rod weighs only slightly over 6 ounces. It has long been used for steelhead and other fresh-water fish, and the Winston Company is now working on a slow-action rod particularly suited for salt-water fly-fishing. The Winston is priced at $75 plus $25 more for the extra tip.

Leonard has long made a grilse rod that suits very well for salt-water fishing. In fact, one of the best rods I ever used was a 9½-foot, 6¾-ounce Leonard grilse rod. I used it for bass-bug fishing, for Atlantic salmon, shad, and stripers. It had everything, and was a pleasure to cast with. Such Leonard rods retail for about $85 with two tips.

Before purchasing a rod for salt-water fly fishing, the angler should personally check to see if it has the desired slow action. To do this, grasp the butt firmly with both hands, and while holding the butt still, impart to the rod

8

a side-to-side swing. If the action comes down too near the butt, you have the rod you need.

If, as is often the case now, you purchase a rod that does not have rustless guides, be sure to have them put on before using the rod in salt water. The regular steel guides will rust rapidly when used in the salt and will eventually go to pieces. Another necessary precaution to protect your rod is to run fresh water over it after each using, and, of course, be sure to dry it before placing it in its case. Wet rods put in aluminum or plastic rod cases may cause the rod sections to become unglued, thereby ruining your stick.

REELS

To function well in salt water, a reel must have several improvements over the usual fresh-water variety. The basic requirement is a single-action fly rod reel with a click and a good dependable drag. The drag is extremely important because in salt-water fly-fishing, where lightning-like speed is encountered, a reel with a faulty, irregular drag will cost you many a good fish.

The reel must be of sturdy construction in order to meet the power, long runs, and lengthy fights put up by salt-water fish. And it must be able to stand the corrosive action of salt fairly well.

For use in salt-water fishing, a reel must also have the capacity to carry from 400 to 600 feet of line. Such a volume of line is seldom needed for fresh-water reels, which, except those used for Atlantic salmon and steelhead, do little more than act as carrying agent for the line. In salt water, however, you meet with fish that tear off 4, 5, and 6 hundred feet of line in one run. There are tales of bonefish and tarpon that never did stop running. They took all the line provided and kept right on. To meet such exigencies, then, the reel must carry the standard casting line of 90 to 105 feet plus a minimum of 100 yards of backing. If the reel will allow it, even more backing is advisable.

The best reel I have ever found for salt-water fly-fishing was one which was manufactured especially for Atlantic salmon. It is the Otto Zwarg, single-action Atlantic salmon reel #2/0 and called by Zwarg "The Sagueney." I used one for an entire winter in Florida waters, with the idea of seeing just how it would take the salt. Until five months had passed I could not detect any lessening of its efficiency, but at the end of six months it was badly in need of oiling. After having it oiled and cleaned, I put it back to work and after another six months it needed another such job but otherwise was in perfect order. An example of the kind of usage it stood should give sufficient illustration of its merits: with this Zwarg reel I fought a 65-pound tarpon for three and one half hours. The big fish took off repeatedly on runs of 600 and 800 feet and we had to follow it with the outboard. It jumped and shook its head until its gill rakers clattered. It made 500-foot runs, one after another, each ending in a surface roll as the fish tried for air, and every roll leading to another run. Eventually the tarpon got off, but the fault was with the angler, not the reel.

Such a satisfactory reel is necessarily fairly expensive, but it is well worth saving for. The Zwarg Sagueney, whose notable performance is described above, sells for about

$75. S. E. Bogdan of Nashua, N. H., manufactures custom-built salt-water fly reels that sell for $30. Tough and with just about the best brake I've even seen, they perform in masterly style and have capacity for all the line you could possible need.

In a lower-price bracket, but still an excellent reel, is the Hardy St. John. This is a good piece of equipment, and has fine workmanship and the capacity for plenty of line. It does not hold up too well under the action of the salt, but still performs creditably. It sells for about $27.50.

In the $15 class, the Pflueger Medalist is by far the best for salt water. It stands the briny very well, and its only fault is that the drag does not give quite the performance I would like. But I understand that the manufacturer is now working on an improvement of this part of the reel.

The L. W. Holmes Company of Oronoque, Connecticut, makes a salt-water fly reel that holds 300 yards of 18-pound test nylon squidding line in addition to the regulation GAF fly-casting line. It is a good reel, too, and sells for $25.

The Langley Company of San Diego, California, also produces a reel, # 176, made for fresh water, but suitable for salt. It sells for $7.25.

Most reel manufacturers are now aware of the increasing interest in salt-water fly-fishing and are already working on improvements to meet its requirements. No doubt within a short time there will be a selection of good salt-water reels at various prices.

Whatever your choice of a reel, it must be remembered that to stand the rugged treatment of salt-water fly-fishing, it should always be in good working order. This is particu-

11

larly true at present, when most reels now being used in the salt are manufactured for fresh water only. The reel should be washed off with fresh water after each salt-water excursion. I hold mine under the tap for several minutes so that the force of the water will wash off any salt or sand that may be clinging to it.

The reel should also be greased and oiled regularly and the drag must be checked frequently, since the drag on most reels, as they are now manufactured, is none too strong. A reel that performs smoothly at all times is well worth a little time and effort expended to keep it in order.

LINES AND BACKING

In all fly-fishing it is highly important that the line be matched to the rod. This is particularly emphasized in salt water, where an underlined rod, combined with the large streamers and poppers used, makes for very slight chances of a good cast.

The ideal salt-water fly line is a forward taper, or, as some anglers call it, a torpedo head. The GAF forward-tapered line, which I prefer, has 8 feet of thin taper in front of an 18- or 25-foot belly (the heaviest part of the line) with the rest of the line made of small, level, running line. For better casting, the end of the line in front of the forward taper section should be cut off about 2½ feet from where the taper begins to thicken.

This line fits most rods from 9 feet up. But for my money it performs best on the 9½-foot rod. The construction of the line works for the angler to make casting easier,

12

Two Bermuda chub caught by the author. These 4-pound fighters really go to town, and the angler knows he has been in a fight before he lands them. *Bermuda News Bureau, Photo by Perinchief.*

Guide Fred Narvel and the author with two fly-rod shad caught on the Susquehanna River below the Conowingo Dam.

JOE BROOKS SALT-WATER STREAMER FLIES

Left: #101, 3/0 hook; center: Joe Brooks Popper, 3/0 hook; right: #105 Bucktail Streamer. Tied by Bill Upperman, Atlantic City, New Jersey. *Photo by Fred Hess & Son.*

and the weight up front helps to carry the large lure out into the wind. For extra long casts with large lures, it can't be topped. You need only pick up 30 feet, cast, and shoot the rest of the line. Shoots of 20 and 30 feet with this line are simple.

The GAF taper also enables you to get out line without excessive false casting. This saves your arm considerably and is priceless in tricky water because of the quickness with which the lure can be presented to an oncoming fish.

Double tapers and level lines are also used by some anglers but for salt-water fly-fishing, neither is in the same league with the GAF. The level line has the weight for a long cast but is almost impossible to shoot, and the double taper is relatively useless under salt water fishing conditions.

The following table will give some idea of the line best suited to certain rods. It should be remembered also that as a general rule, in salt-water fly-fishing, the faster the action of the rod, the heavier the line it will require.

ROD LENGTH	ROD WEIGHT	LINE SIZE
10 feet	7 to 7¼ ounces	GAF or G2AF
9½ feet	6 to 7 ounces	GAF
9 feet	5¾ to 6 ounces	GBF
	6 ounces and over	GAF
8½ feet	4¾ to 5 ounces	HCF
	5 to 5¼ ounces	GBF

The figures quoted are for nylon as nylon lines are lighter and the synthetic material seems to stand up much better than silk under the influence of salt water.

The stretch in nylon is another reason for my preference in this respect. The give of the nylon has saved me many a fish that had wound the line around an obstruction that would have snapped an ordinary line. For the same reasons, nylon is also better for the backing required on the salt-water reel. While I used to use the regular 10-pound test nylon casting line as backing, I have recently changed over to 14-pound test nylon squidding line. I use the 14-pound test so that it will be heavier than the leader. For large tarpon and stripers, I use a 12-pound test tippet on a 10-foot leader, and for bonefish, an 8-pound test tippet—and therefore the backing should be a heavier pound test. Then if anything breaks, it will be the leader and I will lose only the fly. If a lighter weight backing were in use, it might go first, under pressure, in which case casting line, fly, leader, and all are lost.

The casting line requires care both before and after each fishing trip. Before use it should be greased to prevent it from sinking. A sinking line is difficult to handle—heavy to pick up, awkward to play the lure with, slow to strike, and most of all, it upsets the casting. The entire length which you are likely to cast should be greased, and many gadgets to the contrary, the best way to do this is by hand. Dip your fingers lightly in the grease and rub it into the line evenly, taking care to cover all sides. Then wipe the line off with a piece of clean cloth. If superfluous grease stays on the line, it will peel off on the guides and clog them, thus preventing shooting. It will also pick up grit from the bottom of the boat, and this will hasten its sinking.

After use, the line should be washed off with fresh water. I do mine at the same time as I do the reel, simply by holding the whole thing under a good strong faucet.

Then it should be spread to dry or put on one of the regulation driers.

This small amount of care, before and after, will preserve the line so that it will give its full quota of service.

The backing must be checked occasionally, too, for weak spots. Neglect of backing can make for expensive fishing. I have one rather sad illustration in mind. My wife had hooked into her first bonefish and in the excitement she forgot my instructions to leave the reel alone until the fish had finished its run. While it was still traveling at sixty miles per, Mary froze on the reel. Of course something had to give. I heard the *zing!* as it snapped, and waded over to find my wife staring at the broken end of the backing. Somewhere in the Bay of Florida a bonefish is towing a perfectly good casting line, which, to add insult to injury, I had borrowed from my good friend Gordie Dean!

But the point is, if the backing had been perfect, the tippet would have broken first and the line would have been saved.

Lines and backing are produced by many different companies. I have used the Ashaway nylon lines—usually GAF size—produced by the Ashaway Line and Twine Manufacturing Company of Ashaway, R. I. With backing of nylon squidding line manufactured by the same company, this line performs beautifully. Not only does Ashaway GAF cover all casting needs for salt-water fly-fishing, but it holds up and gives good, long usage. And best of all, this line floats well and dries quickly. For an all-around performance, I like the Ashaway lines very much.

The Marathon Line Company of Homer, N. Y., makes

nylon GBF and GAF lines which have done very well, too, as have those manufactured by the Cortland Line Company of Cortland, N. Y. And the Newton Line Company of Homer, N. Y., produces a GAF and a GBF nylon line, both of which have stood the salt water in great style and are noted for their very smooth finish.

These lines all have a length of 30 to 35 yards. The GAF sells for about $11 and the GBF for about $10. For approximately $3 more it is possible to buy the line with 300 feet of backing already spliced on. Having the line spliced to the backing right at the factory saves time and trouble, and the professional job gives you the added assurance that the tie will not let you down.

However, I don't bother with splices. For my own use I tie both the leader to the end of the casting line, and the backing to the other end with a barrel knot. I have found that such a tie is quicker, less expensive, and will hold as long as a professional spliced job. It only takes a short while to make such a join and it will hold for a long time; also, it is small enough to slip through the guides on your rod. It does pay to check where the knot is tied, now and then, but so far I have never had such a tie let me down.

Nylon squidding line for backing costs about $2.30 for a 100-yard spool of 14-pound test, and $2.50 for the 18-pound test.

LEADERS

Every time I tie on a new leader I wonder what we did in the days before nylon appeared. Nylon leaders are made for salt-water fly-fishing They are tough and strong. They do not give off light flashes. They do not kink and they are resilient enough to impart action to the lure.

Nylon leader material comes in a number of sizes, marked according to pound test so that the leader can be tapered by barrel or blood knots to the desired tippet strength. This taper is extremely important and should run from a heavy taper of, say 20-pound test, to 15, to 12, and on down to whatever tippet size you want to use. Be sure to taper gradually because a too-quick taper will bring your fly over too fast. For good casting it is best to have the heavy-pound test to start with or the usually present wind may cause your fly or bug to fall in a bird's nest of spiraled and tangled leader. Stick to the heavy-pound test up top and your casting will benefit immensely.

The finer your leader, of course, the greater the sport. For instance, when fishing for such tackle busters as bone-fish, baby tarpon, and others, it is fun to taper down to 6- or even 4-pound test tippet. Landing these fish on such light tippets takes great skill and represents a fine angling achievement.

A level leader will do the job, of course, but the taper makes for better casting and for a lighter presentation of the fly. The lighter tippet also enables the angler to give better action to the lure.

The over-all length of the leader should be at least 9

feet. This puts the lure farther out from the splash the line makes when it lands on the water. There is less chance of the fish seeing the line in the air, too, and flushing as a consequence. On glassy days when fish are usually scary, it pays to use even greater leader length, up to 12 and 14 feet. The more I fish, the more I am convinced that long and fine leaders take many more fish.

The leader requires a minimum of care but that minimum is extremely important. Knots will cause a leader to break and those which you will occasionally acquire while casting should be cut out at once, and the leader put together again with a barrel knot. It also pays to run your fingers along the leader after a fish has been landed. Nicks and abrasions indicate a weakness, caused either by the fish's teeth or often, as in the case of snook and tarpon, by the hard gill covers. Cut the leader above these abrasions and tie on such lengths as are required for the over-all length you want.

Frequent casts weaken the leader, too, especially where it is tied to the lure. This point on the equipment should be checked often. I make a practice of cutting an inch or so from my leader every now and again, as a safeguard.

All these things take only a minute to do and may save you many a nice fish.

There are many firms selling nylon leader material and several of the companies are now making tapered leaders, some of which are a complete taper sans knots. These cost from 25¢ to 45¢ and are anywhere from 9 to 12 feet long. It is cheaper, of course, to buy coils of leader material in different weight tests and tie your own tapers. When you tie them, using the barrel knot, be sure to add

18

a couple of extra winds around to keep the nylon from slipping. I usually make six or seven winds on each side.

A 10-yard coil of nylon leader material sells for from 15¢ to 25¢, up to 15-pound test. Above that it runs a few cents more. Some of the different companies selling nylon leader material in 10-yard coils and in already prepared tapers are the Mason Tackle Company of Otisville, Michigan; Glen L. Evens, Inc., Caldwell, Idaho; and the Ashaway Line and Twine Manufacturing Company of Ashaway, R. I.

CLOTHING AND WADING GEAR

Clothing of a dull color is a must for salt-water fly-fishing. A white shirt reflects over the water and it is more than likely that the fish can see the white sleeve thrusting back and forth as the angler casts. The same applies to white caps. Khaki shirt, pants, and cap will blend with the outdoor scene and are inconspicuous in clear weather or rough. The shirt should have long sleeves that can be rolled down if the sun is excessive or if sand flies, mosquitoes, and other noxious insects are around.

Most salt-water wading can be done in ordinary tennis shoes, but there are some places where a thick rubber sole is definitely needed. Along the Florida Keys, where the wader will encounter coral formations, such a sole is a necessity for comfort. Leather-soled shoes will slip on the coral while felt soles would be cut to shreds in no time. Regular waders which come to the armpits and have a rubber-boot foot are by far the best gear for ocean use.

Waders are manufactured by most of the large rubber companies and sell for about $20 to $25.

Hip boots are too short for satisfactory wading as they limit you too much to shallow water, and now and again, in wading the flats you may step into a depression which would bring the water over your boot tops.

In the heat of the summer I prefer to wade wet and enjoy the refreshing coolness of the water. A wading shoe which is 14 to 16 inches high is best for wet wading. It will go a long way toward defeating the sand and fine particles of debris, which try to get down between your shoes and your stockings and which can make very painful abrasions on the feet. The jungle boot with a 16-inch canvas top and a rubber composition sole is the best boot of this kind that I have been able to discover. These were procurable for several years after the war, at war-surplus stores, sporting-goods stores, and shoe shops, but have now become rather difficult to find. However, a pair of high tennis shoes with heavy wool socks makes a reasonable substitute. With this foot gear I wear either shorts or longs, in the latter case tucking the trousers into my socks to keep out the sand.

To complete the outfit worn for fishing the shallow salt a pair of Polaroid glasses is a necessity. They add immensely to the ability of the angler to see underwater, and in the shallows it is vastly important to see fish quickly. The popular Polaroid glasses that sell at any drugstore for $1.69 are perfect. This company also makes a curved-lens glass that is slightly more expensive but cuts off any penetration of light from the side.

Particularly in the southern salt, a sun-tan lotion is essential. Of the many different brands I have tried, I have never come across one that does as good a job as Tartan. One application before you start fishing, and another at noon, if you are to be out all day, is generally all that is needed. And if you use it properly you will not get a bad burn. In fact, I have been out on blistering days and as a result of using Tartan have not been slightly burned.

No matter where you fish, you will encounter mosquitoes and sand flies from time to time and it is always well to be prepared for them. There are many kinds of insect repellents on the market, most of them giving some protection from these insidious pests. My preference is for "6-12," and even with that I find that frequent applications are sometimes required, in fly season, to keep the persistent beggars away. But repellents do help, and your favorite brand should be included as part of your fishing gear.

Snakes are a hateful if fascinating subject. But poisonous ones do occur in some of the best fishing spots and should be guarded against. Fishing the canals in Florida, anglers meet the hazard of both the cottonmouth moccasin and the diamondback rattlesnake. Those who wade through the mangroves in search of finny fighters occasionally encounter alligators or crocodiles. But in three years of fishing this area I have only seen a few snakes on the roads and I cannot recall any incident of an angler being struck by a snake. I've seen only one rattler along the canals and it was one that I ran over with my car, on the Flamingo Road. He had sixteen rattles. I've also seen only one cottonmouth during the daytime—a big, repulsive-looking creature that slipped away into the bushes before I could get a good look at him. And while the coral snake is also found in Florida, I discount its threat because the fangs are set so far back in such a small mouth that you would have to be unconscious for the creature to have time to poison you. This strange little snake could not sink its teeth into anything larger than an ear lobe, or perhaps a little finger, and would have to chew its way in, bulldoglike, before it could use the poison fangs.

There is no report of an angler being attacked by an alligator or a crocodile, either. Most of these reptiles believe in "live and let live."

Nevertheless, it pays to be on the alert and case every bit of land you traverse while seeking casting spots along the banks of canals. High, thick boots are a worth-while insurance against snake bite, but constant looking and guarding against becoming careless in your walking is the best bet.

As a final safeguard, carry a snake-bite kit along. There are two very compact ones on the market, one being no bigger than your thumb and the other a 6-inch box. If you do get struck by a snake, use the kit, try to stay calm, and get to a doctor as fast as possible. But by all means avoid panic or needless movement as that only speeds the poison through the blood stream.

BOAT BEHAVIOR

Proper boat behavior is second nature to most veteran anglers, but there are a few points that should be noted by those who have not fished from boats very much, or who are making their first jaunt in salt water.

Everyone knows that for the sake of safety, they should walk and sit in the middle of the boat. This also gives better balance and therefore makes for easier manipulation of the boat. If you are standing to do your casting, get your feet well apart and be sure that they are firmly planted. A solid stance like that will help to avoid a ducking or possibly a bad fall if the boat handler should make a sudden stop or a quick turn.

Remember that the guide works hard to get fish for you. Sometimes he will row or pole throughout a long day, searching for fish. That is hard work and some consideration should be given his comfort. Sit down when he is moving the boat from one location to another. He will keep a lookout so you won't miss any fish, and you will offer less wind resistance. Guides are eager to have you enjoy your sport and it helps the team if you do your part.

Before fly casting from a boat, it pays to clear decks of loose objects that might interfere with the line. In some skiffs the bottom slats end several feet from the bow and stern and offer a perfect trap for excess line. Invariably, when you make your cast and start your shoot, the free line will wind around those floor boards and ruin your effort. There are many other contrivances about a skiff that seem to conspire against you—wooden splinters, oarlocks, extra rod cases, oars, gas cans, outboards, and other duffle—either part of the boat's equipment, or brought along by the angler.

The angler should decide from just which point he is going to cast and then clean things up around him where he is apt to drop excess line as he strips in his fly. Most shallow-water fly casters stand in the bow with rod in hand, line ready coiled or dropped loosely on the bottom, ready to make a cast to a fish. Others prefer to sit down when casting from a boat. I like to stand because I can see farther and spot more fish more quickly, and thus get off a cast before the fish see me. The higher position makes for better casting and better lure play and allows you to follow the course of the fish and see the strike. Perhaps the fish sees you sooner, too, but it seems to me that the deal is in the angler's favor.

When you are casting to a fish, it is hard to give much thought to anything else—but watch that backcast! I've seen many guides hit by wild swinging flies. While the sting of the hook may not amount to much, there is always the danger of catching the guide or a fellow passenger in the eye.

When approaching a fish, make as few extra motions as possible. Try to get the lure out with a minimum of false casts. Quick and frequent motions will attract the attention of the fish and probably frighten them off.

Noise will scare fish, too. Talking in ordinary tones doesn't bother fish, as they receive their hearing impressions from the water through their lateral lines. From that point the sound vibrations are carried along the numerous nerves running to the ear stones. Thus the sound has to originate where it can be carried by the water, in order to reach them. That's why the sound of a pole grating on the bottom—a sound scarcely audible to the angler—will flush a bonefish or send a tarpon off in a wild flight, while a shout would probably not disturb them at all. Avoid all noises on the sides or bottom of the boat. Don't scrape tackle boxes across the bottom or knock the oars against the sides. Wear tennis shoes and walk like a cat. It will mean more chances of fish.

LINE PLAY

There are many ways to handle line when retrieving a lure, but to my mind the strip method is by far the most efficient. Simply grasp the rod in the right hand with the thumb and index finger sticking out from the inside part of the rod grip. When ready to start the retrieve, take the line between these two fingers, pick up the line behind them in your left hand and pull it back a foot, loosening the thumb and index finger of the right hand as you do so. After each foot-long strip, tighten again with the fingers, repeating this procedure until you are ready to pick up the line for the next cast. That way, you can play the lure fast or slow or with a series of quick strips or long slow ones, and at all times you will have a tight line and be ready for the strike. In addition to being in a position to strike easily, you will be able to pick up your line with dispatch, thus getting a good backcast. Most other ways of retrieving are not mobile enough, allow for slack, limit you to a certain speed, and just don't begin to compare to the strip method.

Many northern trout fishermen, used to fishing in small streams, retrieve by manipulation of the fingers, making a figure 8 of the retrieved line in the palm of the hand. In an effort to catch up on the slack as the fly gets closer, the angler then starts moving his rod back until sometimes it is pointing behind him, in the opposite direction to the original cast. Trying to strike a fish from that position is hopeless. But with the strip way of doing it, your rod is pointed in the direction of the lure, there is no slack, and you are always ready to strike.

2.

Lures

A<small>LTHOUGH</small> during the past three years many salt-water flies have been fashioned and have proved to be fish getters, there is as yet no book available that lists salt-water fly patterns.

The first fly-rod anglers in the tidal waters used fresh-water flies. Dr. Henshall mentions catching ladyfish on bass flies as far back as 1897 and the angler, previously described in this book as catching shad on the Susquehanna River in 1876, used trout flies. When Tom Loving began catching brackish-water largemouth black bass in 1922, he used streamers, bucktails, and popping bugs that he made himself, especially for that fishing. The next year he tied a two-hooked fly for shad, made with white bucktail wings and a black body with silver ribbing. As far as I know, that was the real beginning of salt-water fly tying.

Right on top of that, Tom made a large white streamer fly with a red neck hackle, for striped bass. I remember very well the first newspaper account of his trip to the Severn River and the seven stripers he took in one afternoon with that fly. They weighed from 6 to 21 pounds. It was only a month after that when I took my first journey to the salt with Tom.

Later, in Florida waters, several pioneering anglers got really serious about tying on artificial fly-rod foolers for salt-water fish. Howard Bonbright evolved the Bonbright Tarpon Fly. He caught tarpon at once with it and it still is a very hot number for the acrobatic Mr. Silver King.

Around the same time, Homer Rhode, Jr., of Miami, used his experience in tying fresh-water flies to fashion lures that took salt-water game fish. His familiarity with Florida waters helped him to tie fine imitations of the underwater life upon which those fish fed. Later, H. J. (Red) Greb, also of Miami, started making salt-water streamers, popping bugs, and wounded minnows, and was, as far as I have been able to find out, the first man to tie a fly especially for bonefish.

Eight or nine years ago, Dick Splaine was tying salt-water flies and gradually, from his earlier attempts, evolved the "squeteaguer," which has proved so deadly on sea trout. Dick's was not the first tandem fly to be tied, but it was developed through watching huge sea trout strike at the head of the fly. He was missing strikes and his keen observation told him why. He tied on a head hook and immediately began catching fish.

Three years ago, Gordon M. Dean produced the now well-known bead-head fly. He placed a small wooden bead at the head of the fly and came up with one of the prettiest streamers I have ever seen. They are now being tied commercially by Lacey Gee, of the Wapsi Company of Independence, Iowa. Not to be outdone, I put my oar in and designed an entire line of salt-water streamer flies, buck-tails, and poppers. Tied on Z nickle hooks that do not rust, they are tough, well made, and fish go for them in a big way. They are the result of years of experimenting, and are proved fish getters. Bill Upperman of Atlantic City, New Jersey, ties them commercially.

Sometime during those early days, the breather type of fly was evolved. The saddle hackles, used as wings, were tied with several hackles on each side of the hook, with the hackles flared outward. As you retrieve them in foot-long jerks, the hackles go together. Then, when you stop the strip, they flare out, giving action that is very lifelike. Harry Friedman, of Miami, went even further than this. He picked the longest saddle hackles he could get, matched them carefully, put four or five hackles on each side of the hook, and had a fly 5 inches long that was irresistible to tarpon and snook. His method of tying the hackles on also gave strength and beauty to the fly. Instead, of stripping the thin webbing off at the butt end of the hackle, which weakens it, he left it on, and when tied on the hook, it made the whole tie stronger and also gave the appearance of more body at that point. He used chenille bodies and some of his patterns have a marabou feather on either side of the hook for more action, and some have jungle-cock eyes. The Mad River Tackle Shop of Ossining, N. Y., tie a line of salt-water flies and popping bugs that are well made, tough, and with plenty of fish appeal.

Outstanding among the northern fly tyers, Frank and Harold Gibbs of Rhode Island each tied a striper fly that had what it takes to bring strikes from that fish. Harold has taken over 800 stripers with his model and Frank has done almost as well with his. They are particularly good flies with small stripers.

Hook size is as important as all get out in salt-water flies. A light hook is needed when fishing in the thin water of the flats, as a heavy one will sink too quickly and catch on the bottom. A 1/0 hook is about right for this kind of water, and in an effort to get even more lightness, some of the manufacturers are making them with short shanks. The length of the hook doesn't matter much, but the lightness is essential.

For some other types of fishing, a heavier hook is best. I use a 3/0 Z nickle hook for both tarpon and snook as it gets the fly down to them so much more quickly than the 1/0 does.

Because they do not rust, the Z nickle hooks are by far the best for salt-water fishing. They keep their strength, and do not deteriorate like most other hooks. Nor do they transfer rust to the feathers of other lures in your box.

By trial and error, a few color combinations are beginning to stand out, and slowly, certain standard fly patterns are emerging. While most salt-water fish will hit any old lure at one time or another, there are days when they are not so eager, and that is the time that the tested lures pay off. Those outstanding favorites in fresh water, red and yellow and red and white, are beginning to show in salt-water patterns, too, as are wings of barred rock or domenicker. Plain bucktail in white or yellow, with red winding at the head, makes another good all-around lure.

The bucktail tied by Upperman, of Atlantic City, was the outcome of my first experimenting with bonefish. Since they seemed to feed almost exclusively on crustaceans, I tried for a fly to represent shrimp. I arrived at a palmer-tied ginger-hackle affair with brown and white wings. It worked well. Then I tried about every other fly I could dream up and they all seemed to work equally well at some time or another. When I started to tie them on short-shanked Z nickle hooks, they worked even better. Finally I tied a white bucktail with a red head on a 1/0 hook, and took five fish with it in a row. After that I fished white bucktail almost exclusively until spring, when, finding that they seemed to be becoming a little leery of it, I changed to feathers and had immediate response. Thereafter, I used white bucktails during the winter months and around the first of May turned to streamers. So, throughout my fly box I have narrowed down the patterns to a few that will give me consistently good fishing throughout the year.

There are so many flies tied by individuals for their own use that it would be impossible to list all of them. But since only a few companies are tying salt-water flies commercially, I will endeavor to list those. They can be purchased in most sporting-goods stores and you can be sure that they are well made, tough, and have the right hooks and color combinations for those strong, salt-water scrappers. They are also lures that I have tried and found from my own experience to be good, steady fish producers.

Though many of them have never been officially named, beyond "streamer fly," "bucktail," or "popping bug," the patterns supplied will help the purchaser to decide what he wants, and will also assist those who wish to tie their own flies.

PATTERNS

Upperman Joe Brooks Streamer Flies

# 101	Hook	1/0 Z nickle
	Body	white chenille
	Wings	white saddle hackle, 3½ inches long; 3 or 4 on either side of hook
	Hackle	red

Used for bonefish, ladyfish, spotted sea trout, sea trout, jack crevalle, baby tarpon, bluefish.

Same fly (101) tied on 3/0 hook with 4½-inch wings used for spotted sea trout, sea trout, barracuda, striped bass, snook, channel bass, brackish-water largemouth black bass, tarpon over 15 pounds, bluefish.

# 103	Hook	1/0 Z nickle
	Body	black chenille
	Wings	yellow saddle hackle, 3½ inches long; 3 or 4 on either side of hook
	Hackle	red

Used for bonefish, ladyfish, jack crevalle, baby tarpon, mackerel.

Same fly (103) tied on 3/0 hook with 4½-inch wings used for spotted sea trout, sea trout, barracuda, striped bass, snook, channel bass, brackish-water largemouth black bass, tarpon over 15 pounds.

# 107	Hook	1/0 Z nickle
	Body	yellow chenille
	Wings	brown and yellow saddle hackles, 3½ inches long; 2 of each color on either side of hook
	Hackle	yellow

Used for bonefish, baby tarpon, ladyfish, spotted sea trout, jack crevalle.

Same fly (107) tied on 3/0 hook with 4½-inch wings used for striped bass, tarpon over 15 pounds, snook, channel bass, mackerel.

# 104	Hook	1/0 Z nickle
	Body	white chenille
	Wings	barred rock saddle hackle, 3½ inches long; 3 or 4 on either side of hook
	Hackle	yellow

Used for bonefish, baby tarpon, ladyfish, bluefish.

Same fly (104) tied on 3/0 with 4½-inch wings used for jack crevalle, striped bass, snook, channel bass, brackish-water largemouth black bass, tarpon over 15 pounds, bluefish, mackerel.

# 102	Hook	1/0 Z nickle
	Body	black chenille
	Wings	yellow saddle hackle, 3½ inches long; 3 or 4 on either side of hook
	Hackle	yellow

Used for bonefish, baby tarpon, ladyfish.

Same fly (102) tied on 3/0 hook with 4½-inch wings used for snook, tarpon over 15 pounds, channel bass.

# 108	Hook	1/0 Z nickle
	Body	yellow chenille
	Wings	white saddle hackle, 3½ inches long; 3 or 4 on either side of hook
	Hackle	gray

Used for bonefish, ladyfish, snapper, black bass, sea trout, spotted sea trout, baby tarpon, bluefish.

Salt Water Fly Fishing

Same fly (108) tied on 3/0 hook with 4½-inch wings used for tarpon over 15 pounds, snook, sea trout, spotted sea trout, channel bass, black bass, striped bass.

Upperman Joe Brooks Bucktails

# 105	Hook	1/0 Z nickle
	Wings	white bucktail, divided, 3 inches long
	Head	red silk winding

Used for bonefish, ladyfish, bluefish.

Same fly (105) on 3/0 hook with 4-inch bucktail used for spotted sea trout, sea trout, striped bass, channel bass, snook, barracuda.

# 106	Hook	1/0 Z nickle
	Wings	yellow bucktail, divided, 3 inches long
	Head	yellow silk winding

Used for bonefish, ladyfish, snapper.

Same fly (106) tied on 3/0 hook with 4-inch bucktail used for spotted sea trout, sea trout, striped bass, channel bass, snook, mackerel, barracuda.

Upperman Joe Brooks Popping Bugs

White	Hook	1/0 Z nickle
	Body	white balsa wood, 1 inch long, round, flat face
	Tail	white bucktail, 2 inches long

Used for ladyfish, baby tarpon, brackish-water largemouth black bass.

Same pattern tied on 3/0 hook with 1½-inch body and 3-inch tail used for spotted sea trout, sea trout, barracuda, jack crevalle, striped bass, snook, channel bass, brackish-water largemouth black bass, tarpon (over 15 pounds).

34

Yellow	Hook	1/0 Z nickle
	Body	yellow balsa wood, 1 inch long, round, flat face
	Tail	yellow bucktail, 2 inches long

Used for ladyfish, baby tarpon, brackish-water largemouth black bass.

Same pattern tied on 3/0 hook with 1½-inch body and 3-inch tail used for spotted sea trout, sea trout, barracuda, jack crevalle, striped bass, snook, channel bass, brackish-water largemouth black bass, tarpon over 15 pounds.

Upperman Joe Brooks Shad Fly

	Hook	# 2
	Body	white chenille, weighted, silver tinsel ribbing
	Wing	white bucktail, sparse

Used for shad and hickory shad.

Wapsi Company Gordon Dean Bead Head Flies

The Ruby Throat	Hook	1/0 Z nickle
	Body	white
	Wings	white
	Hackle	red
	Head	white bead

Used for bonefish, ladyfish, channel bass, baby tarpon, barracuda, snapper, bluefish.

The Topper	Hook	1/0 Z nickle
	Body	yellow
	Wings	brown and yellow
	Hackle	yellow
	Head	black bead

Used for bonefish, baby tarpon, barracuda.

Salt Water Fly Fishing

The Skippy	Hook	1/0 Z nickle
	Body	silver tinsel
	Wings	yellow, 3½ inches long
	Hackle	red
	Head	yellow bead

Used for spotted sea trout, sea trout, baby tarpon, bonefish, barracuda, snapper.

The Yellow Grizzly	Hook	1/0 Z nickle
	Body	silver tinsel
	Wings	yellow and grizzly
	Head	yellow bead

Used for snook, baby tarpon, barracuda, mackerel, bluefish, snapper.

The Silver Grizzly	Hook	1/0 Z nickle
	Body	silver tinsel
	Wings	white and grizzly
	Hackle	black
	Head	white bead

Used for channel bass, baby tarpon, snook.

Dick Splaine's Squeteaguer

Head hook	1/0
Tail hook	1/0
Head	black with yellow eye
Body	white bucktail with three 5-inch dun saddle hackles roofed; entire fly tied on head hook; single shank of 15-pound test nylon leader material goes from head hook to tail hook; 2-inch length of # 5 wire in front of fly, with standard # 1 silver spinner

Used for spotted sea trout, sea trout.

Dick Splaine's Treble Hook Sea Trout Fly

Hook	size 1, treble
Body	white bucktail with two flared white saddle hackles, all tied on end of wire; 3-inch length of # 5 wire in front of fly with standard # 1 silver spinner
Hackle	red

Used for spotted sea trout, sea trout.

Howard Bonbright Tarpon Fly

Hook	5/0
Body	silver tinsel
Wings	white feather, 2½ inches long
Cheek	jungle cock over red rib
Tag	red and white topping
Hackle	white

Used for tarpon over 15 pounds.

Same pattern tied on 3/0 or 1/0 hook used for baby tarpon.

Polly Rosborough Tarpon Fly (The Silver Garland)

Hook	3/0 Z nickle
Body	silver tinsel, weighted
Wings	white marabou, blue on top
Head	black, with white eye

Used for tarpon over 15 pounds.

Connecticut River Shad Fly # 1

Red bead ahead of hook

Hook	1/0
Body	flat silver tinsel
Wing	red dyed duck feather, ¼ inch wide, tied upright at middle of shank

Used for shad and hickory shad.

37

Connecticut River Shad Fly # 2

Red bead ahead of hook
Hook	1/0
Body	flat silver tinsel
Wing	orange dyed duck feather, ¼ inch wide, 1¼-inch long
Tail	orange dyed duck feather, 1 inch long

Used for shad and hickory shad.

Dillon's Shad Fly

Hook	# 8, long
Body	white chenille with silver tinsel ribbing
Wings	white bucktail or white hackle
Tail	golden pheasant tippet

Used for shad and hickory shad.

Pacific Coast Shad Fly (McCredie Special)

Hook	2X, short
Body	red wool, gold tinsel ribbing
Wing	black bucktail, 1¼ inches long
Hackle	white bucktail, 2 inches long, under hook
Head	black

Used for shad.

The Harold Gibbs Fly

Hook	# 4, long shanked, turned-down eye
Body	silver, no tag
Wings	3-inch white bucktail, fairly full

| | 1½-inch bright blue feather as cheek, tapering to point, each side; shorter cheek (tied over blue feather) of brown feather with white rib, ¼ inch long |
| Head | painted yellow eyes with small black dot for pupil |

Used for striped bass.

The Frank Gibbs Fly

Hook	# 4 Sproat, turned-down eye
Body	silver
Wings	4-inch wide impali, tied full, white; atop the white impali, 3-inch red bucktail; 3-inch barred rock hackle feather on each side; shorter cheek (tied over hackle feather) of brown with white rib, ¼ inch long
Head	painted white eyes with red dot for pupil

Used for striped bass.

Spinner-Fly Combinations

Joe Brooks Streamer # 101 with 1/0 silver spinner used for bonefish, ladyfish, spotted sea trout, sea trout, jack crevalle, baby tarpon, snook, channel bass.

Joe Brooks Streamer # 101, tied on 3/0 hook, with 4½-inch wing, with 1/0 silver spinner, used for spotted sea trout, sea trout, barracuda, striped bass, snook, channel bass, brackish-water largemouth black bass, tarpon over 15 pounds, jack crevalle.

Salt Water Fly Fishing

Joe Brooks Streamer # 103 with 1/0 silver spinner used for bonefish, ladyfish, spotted sea trout, sea trout, jack crevalle, baby tarpon, snook, channel bass.

Joe Brooks Streamer # 103 tied on 3/0 hook, with 4½-inch wing, used for spotted sea trout, sea trout, barracuda, striped bass, snook, channel bass, brackish-water largemouth black bass, tarpon over 15 pounds, jack crevalle.

Joe Brooks Streamer # 104 with 1/0 silver spinner used for bonefish, ladyfish, spotted sea trout, sea trout, jack crevalle, baby tarpon, snook, channel bass.

Joe Brooks Streamer # 104 tied on 3/0 hook with 4½-inch wing, used for spotted sea trout, sea trout, barracuda, striped bass, snook, channel bass, brackish-water largemouth black bass, tarpon over 15 pounds, jack crevalle.

Spoon-Type Lures

OO Huntington Drone
OO Metalure
Trix Orena
Johnson's Gold Minnow # 1030

All four used for shad, brackish-water largemouth black bass, pompano, ladyfish, spotted sea trout, sea trout, snook.

Popping Bugs

Peck's Water Witch
Loving's Gerbubblebug

Both used for brackish-water largemouth black bass.

Hair Bugs

Austin's Jaylures

Used for brackish-water largemouth black bass.

40

BERMUDA FLIES AND LURES

Upperman Joe Brooks Bucktails

# 1A	Hook	3/0 Z nickle
	Wings	white bucktail, tandem 4 inches long
	Head	red silk winding
# 2A	Hook	3/0 Z nickle
	Wings	yellow bucktail, tandem 4 inches long
	Head	yellow silk winding

Both used for bonefish, barracuda, mackerel, sennet.

Upperman Joe Brooks Popping Bugs

# 1A	Hook	3/0 Z nickle
	Body	white balsa wood, 1½ inches long; round, flat face
	Tail	white bucktail, 3 inches long
# 2A	Hook	3/0 Z nickle
	Body	yellow balsa wood, 1½ inches long; round, flat face
	Tail	yellow bucktail, 3 inches long

Both used for barracuda.

Special Bucktails

# 1	Hook	# 2 or # 4, long shank
	Body	none
	Wings	white bucktail with peacock herl on top

# 2	Hook	# 2 or # 4, long shank
	Body	none
	Wings	white bucktail, blue and green dyed bucktail on top
# 3	Hook	# 2 or # 4, long shank
	Body	none
	Wings	white bucktail with blue dyed bucktail top

All used for pompano, yellowtail, bonito, snapper, chub, bream.

Spoon-Type Lures

Trix Orena
OO Huntington Drone
OO Metalure

All used for pompano, yellowtail, bonito.

3.

Brackish-Water Largemouth Black Bass

WHILE thousands of anglers know about the largemouth black bass in fresh water, it has only been during the past fifteen or twenty years that many sportsmen have gone after him in brackish water. In my own case, I had taken largemouth in sweet water for years, but not until 1923, when Tom Loving told me about the catches he was making in the half-salt, did I begin to fish for them there.

I'll never forget that first trip with Tom. We journeyed out to Frog Mortar, an arm of the Chesapeake Bay. Tom toted an outboard and we rented a skiff. The Chesapeake and its tributary streams form one of the country's great ducking areas and as we steamed out from the dock, Tom headed straight for the nearest blind. Now, months after ducking season, practically all that remained was the framework. But there was enough of that to provide plenty of cover for the largemouth. Tom shut off the motor while we were still well out, took up the oars and quietly eased me in toward the blind.

"Be very quiet," he said. "They scare easy—and throw that bug as far as you can."

He stopped the boat about 50 feet away from the blind and I dropped one of his own famous Gerbubble Bugs a foot away from its edge. It had hardly hit before the surface splashed apart and I was fast to a nice fish. I brought him in after a fight that made me marvel at the spirit of those brackish-water bass. He was strong and he just didn't want to quit.

That trip was a revelation. We'd take turns casting to duck blinds. And since the blinds were spaced about every 500 yards, we had plenty of choice fishing. I don't remember how many we took, but a glance through my old scrapbook shows us each holding up two fish that look well over 4 pounds apiece—the only ones we kept. After that I was a confirmed brackish-water angler.

The bass in the half-salt respond wonderfully to a popping bug, fight as hard if not harder than the fresh-water variety, grow to large sizes, and as a whole seem more numerous and healthy. In fact I think that the brackish-water bass is just about as hardy as any fish I've ever encountered. I remember one instance in particular, when Nelson Edwards and I were working on a color movie. We wanted a close-up of a big bass, a full screen shot showing him opening and closing his mouth. Our plan was to have it look as if the bass were talking, telling the story of what happened. But all that day we took only small fish. Finally, at six P.M., we caught a 5-pounder—and the light was insufficient for a color shot!

Ordinarily I wouldn't treat a bass this way, but we were desperate. We put him on a stringer until we were ready to head back, then took him in the power boat, stopping now and again to immerse him in the water to revive him.

44

John Alden Knight, well-known fly caster and creator of the Solunar Tables, holds up a snook he caught in the 10,000 Islands section of the Everglades. *Photo by Chas. C. Ebbets.*

Sunset and the end of a day's largemouth black bass fishing on a brackish-water marsh. *Photo by Chas. C. Ebbets.*

A brackish-water largemouth black bass is put back to strike again some other day. Frog Mortar, an arm of Chesapeake Bay, provides fine largemouth fishing and boasts numerous duck blinds under which the big lunkers lurk and from which they rise to a popping bug.

When we got to the dock, we tied him to it on a stringer, overnight. In the morning, when the sun was bright, we took him off the stringer and I held him in my hands while Nelson made shots of the fish slowly opening and closing his big mouth. Then we put him back in the water and watched him swim away!

Altogether, the largemouth is an admirable character with plenty of backbone, and being so widespread in habitat, is the particular *pièce de résistance* of the sportsman who cannot go very far afield. He is a great fish on any light tackle, and on a fly rod is at his very best because the light lure used does not prohibit his efforts to escape and allows him to wage his best fight.

Since they are scattered along the coastal areas of both the Atlantic and the Pacific Oceans, brackish-water bass make a lot of fishing. They are of the same species, *huro salmoides*, as the largemouth black bass found in fresh-water ponds, lakes, and rivers, but although they have adapted themselves very well to the tidewater, an infusion of too much salt will kill them at once. The most vivid example of this with which I am familiar occurred at Currituck Sound, North Carolina, in 1935 when the ocean broke through the narrow sand belt which separates the sound from the sea. Bass died by the thousands. Since then they have come back, however, and Currituck again offers some really great fishing. The fact that the state of North Carolina has put them on the game-fish list has also helped tremendously in restoring the species. Now, when commercial netters take them in their haul, they put them back into the water unharmed.

Another sballow-water hazard that affects largemouth

and occasionally depletes their ranks is the blooming or seeding of underwater growths. Then, carbonic acid is created and when the blooming coincides with a hot, dry spell, causing the oxygen content to decrease, many bass will die. Although a good hard rain will overcome this condition, and of course a lot of bass escape it by moving out to deeper water, it is nevertheless the cause, now and then, of the premature death of many thousands of bass. During that seeding or blooming period, fishing naturally drops off.

The shallow water in which they feed (water from 2 to 5 feet deep) makes the fly outfit ideal for fishing for large-mouth. At that depth, larger and heavier lures splash and cause so much water disturbance that they often scare the fish away. Not so the lightly dropped fly-rod lures. Even the popping bug, if it lands quietly on the surface and is allowed to rest a while, doesn't frighten the bass, when popped. In fact you can make a fish mad that way, and if you pop the bug long enough and close enough to him, he will get so worked up that he will tear out and sock it mightily.

Like any other fish, brackish-water bass should be fished for in the spots where they shelter and rest and where they feed. Give the go-by to flat or dead water where there is nothing but a smooth, sandy, or muddy bottom, with no hiding places, no shelter for them, and even less for the food upon which they prey. Look for them, instead, under docks and under boats moored in shallow water. Look for them under grass patches and alongside and under logs. During the summer, when the water is hot, they will be found in almost any place that affords some shade. They particularly like to slink under a duck blind or loaf alongside one in the shadows. And the same goes for piles or stakes jutting up from the water. Just a narrow band of shade is enough to shelter a big bass.

Like people, bass prefer to sit out the heat of the day in a shady spot, but you can make them hit at that time, just the same. Pick a likely looking place, where experience has shown that bass should be, and cast your lure in time and again. If a bass is there, he will finally get mad and take a crack at it. Even if you feel sure that old "bigmouth" is not around, repeated casts to such spots will pay off. Once, at Currituck Sound, Nelson Edwards and I were trying to get a motion-picture shot of a bass hitting a popping bug. Nelson set up business on top of a dock where the water was as bassy looking as could be. I took my position in the boat about 50 feet out, and started dropping the popper on the surface where Nelson had his camera trained. I had guaranteed him a strike, but after thirty casts I quit counting and only pure stubbornness kept me throwing the lure in there. But, believe it or not, eventually a bass did come up and wallop that bug! And I can remember many other times when bass got mad much quicker.

Charlie Gillet and I had a ringside seat for some spectacular bass fishing one hot summer day in 1945. We were on the Bush River in Maryland. The water was glassy-still and it was the middle of the day. We told each other that we were slightly insane to be trying to catch bass in such heat and at that time. But we kept trying. At last we hit a shallow, grassy bay where there were sandy holes amid the grass, and as we eased in close, we spotted bass. It was like looking through plate glass and we could clearly see every movement against the light-colored bottom. Every so often a fish would surface. We couldn't see what they were feeding on and as a matter of fact we never did find out, but from the wide dispersal of the fish it must have been a fly hatch and they must have been feeding on the nymph as it neared or just as it reached the surface. We couldn't spot any flies in the air.

Since the water was only about 3 feet deep and very slick, we tied on 4-pound test tippets to our leaders, making them about 12 feet long. It looked as if small bugs were called for, so we put on a Spouter about an inch long, tied on a # 1-3X hook.

Charlie started casting and threw to a bass about 50 feet away. As the line and lure hung over the water ready to drop, we saw the bass dart away. Letting the bug lie where it had landed, Charlie turned to me.

"Imagine that!" he said. "That bass flushed when the bug was still in the air. Scary, eh?"

Just then I saw that bass turn and come for the bug like a gourmet headed for New Orleans. "Charlie, look out!" I shouted. "He's going to hit you!"

Charlie jumped and automatically set the hook as the bass hit, going full speed ahead. Out he came, and Charlie fought him back and finally landed a 3-pounder.

It was my turn then, and Charlie rowed me within range of another bass. I tossed my bug to him and watched him dash wildly away from it.

"I wonder what he'd do if I popped it?" I said.

"Try," answered Charlie.

I gave the bug a pop and the bass put on added speed

48

and disappeared into a distant grass patch. He never did show again. That was enough for me. When the next bass I cast to also ducked out of his feeding place, I let the bug lie quietly on the surface. We watched the bass slow up, turn, and look back toward the bug. I gave it a slight twitch and that fish went for it like lightning. He covered the 10-foot stretch in a second and hit so hard that he jarred my hands. He was smaller than Charlie's fish, but put on a splendid series of jumps.

Between us, we took sixteen bass before the fireworks were over. Each one of them took off at the sight of the line in the air, then came back to hit the bug when it was motionless on the surface. They were so hungry that even after they had been scared they couldn't resist having a go at what they evidently thought was a big moth or a downed insect of some sort. But there is no doubt in either Charlie's or my mind that if we had popped our bugs right back, we wouldn't have had a strike.

Especially during the summer months, bass like a slow-played lure. Most bass fishermen will recall many strikes to motionless surface lures, while their attention was attracted elsewhere. So make the cast and allow the lure to lie still on the surface for about half a minute. Then give it a pop. Let it rest again for about the same length of time before starting the retrieve. Then bring it slowly out, popping it continuously, until you lift it for the backcast. Sometimes it pays to give it three or four pops before even starting the retrieve. Generally, if a bass is going to strike at all, he hits before the lure is a yard or so away from the bank, pile, dock, or whatever you are casting toward. But now and again they will cross you up, and it pays to fish the lure all the way in. Quite often one will hit just as you are about to lift the lure from the water for the next cast. They catch you by surprise every time on this, and invariably you have slack line and can't put home the steel with the required dispatch. As far as I have been able to discover, there is just nothing to be done about that particular situation, unless you have the patience to continue the strip until you come to the leader—but that is a job for Job and not for a fisherman!

While I have occasionally caught brackish-water bass when there was a ripple on the surface, they seldom strike when there is much top-water motion. A popper will bring more strikes in the calm water on a lee shore than along a shoreline where waves are breaking or even where there is a ripple of any sort. My experience has been that fishing surface lures on the lee water will bring 75 per cent more strikes than fishing rippled water. However, when the tide is moving fast enough to form a current, they will hit a bug even when the surface is marred by wind. Usually it is alongside a dock or wharf, or maybe it will be in the holes between islands, or off a point, or beside a grass patch. Points are especially good, wind or no wind; the fish will lie there waiting for food to sweep along to them. They follow the same practice in guts or narrow waterways through the salty marshes. Where such a waterway opens out into the river, there is usually a deep hole where the bottom has been swept clean of mud by tidal action, and in those places bass will be found waiting for food to move in and out.

Charlie Gillet and I fished one of those guts in the Bush River on one of the hottest August afternoons in Maryland weather history. We decided that it would be hopeless to try for largemouth out under the blazing sun and that our best bet would be to cruise slowly up the gut, casting in the shade of overhanging grasses and bushes. We eased along, working our bugs very slowly. Nothing happened for about an hour; then Charlie landed two largemouths, each of which looked as if it would tip the scales at about 4 pounds. A little later I latched onto a 3½-pounder. All three were taken when we had cast and cast repeatedly back to the same spots in the shade under overhanging bushes. None of the hits came before at least ten casts in the same place.

As we came out, Charlie said that we should be able to take a couple from the hole at the end of the gut where it opened into a large, shallow bay. The tide was moving in fast as we reached the spot and as Charlie cast his bug out, the current carried it back toward the gut. Immediately a big, dark shape rose up and knocked the bug a foot into the air. That big bass ignored the next few casts and then, just when we were ready to give up, he had it good. Charlie struck and the fight was on, and eventually a 5-pound fish was landed.

Considering the midsummer heat, that was good fishing —and if we had gone out and fished the shallow water around the tuckahoes and weed patches, the chances are that we would have wound up without a fish.

In the fall, when the water cools off, the bass respond with more vigor. Then they will hit a faster retrieve and their fight is undoubtedly stronger. During the autumn they often move out into deeper water, hanging around floating bits of vegetation and cruising the water beyond the dropoffs. It seems to me that bass feed harder than ever in the fall, storing up energy in their bodies to tide them through the cold winter when they are in a semi-dormant condition and do little if any eating. As a matter of fact, they seem so hungry in the fall that you just can't retrieve too fast. The summer technique of slow retrieves and long, quiet spells when the bug is motionless on the water is definitely out. They want action.

Quite a different system is required when using a streamer fly or a bucktail-spinner combination, both of which are effective largemouth lures on a fly rod. A silver spoon in the OO size is also a very deadly weapon at times. You cast these lures, which are meant to represent minnows, into the same place as you would a bass bug. Allow them to sink a bit and then bring them back in whatever kind of retrieve you think best. Some anglers use a fairly fast retrieve, with foot-long jerks, while others prefer a slow, steady one. So far as I have been able to judge, it is a matter of trial and error; some days the bass seem to like a slow retrieve and at other times they like the speed of a fast bring-back.

When fishing for brackish-water bass, there are always lots of hazards and the angler has to employ every trick he knows to avoid dropping the lure in weed patches or coming up with a trail of grass. You can cast over upthrusting weeds and by making a fast retrieve keep the lure from catching on them. Then, when you hit a deeper spot where there is a hole in the weeds, you can slow the retrieve and in that manner pick up a lot of bass which you might miss by hitting only the easy spots. If there seems to be any possibility of catching fish, however difficult the place you want to drop that lure, give it a whirl anyway. The worst that can happen is that you will hang up on the weeds and have to go over and free your lure—which, of course, means that you put down any fish in that vicinity. But that is part of the game.

In shallow water the rod should be held high as the lure is retrieved. If it is traveling lanes that are close to bass, they will come for it with a rush.

Small spoons are especially good in the spring or early summer before underwater vegetation has taken hold. The weight of the lure takes it down quickly, and while not so good when the grasses have bloomed in the late summer, it really does a fine job in the early part of the bass season. Bass are not so scary then and the flash of the lure seems to attract them from quite a distance. For the spoon-type lures, the retrieve that has been most effective for me is a fairly fast one, with foot-long jerks continued to within 15 feet of the boat.

When the water is still cold enough to keep the fish from hitting on top, you can cash in with your underwater lures. The good old reliable OO Huntington drone saved the day for Jack Knight, Charlie Gillet, and me on a trip to Currituck Sound. The water was too cold for poppers and we tried fly-spinner combinations and took a few fish. Then Charlie discovered a drone in his fly box and tied it on. He connected on his first try and from then on he kept getting strikes and landing bass, while Jack and I had only fair success with other lures.

The regular bass wet flies don't do so well on largemouth unless they are attached to a spinner. Then they are excellent indeed, and after 30 years of bass fishing, I still like to put on a silver 3/0 spinner in front of that first bass fly I ever used, the Professor. It's a good combination, all right, and once on Nanjamoy Creek, near Port Tobacco, Maryland, I saw Frank Bentz make a day of memorable fishing with that setup.

Frank, who was then public-relations man for the Maryland Game and Inland Fish Commission, is a master performer with the bass fly-spinner combination. On the trip I am describing, we were fishing with his son, Frank Jr., and Bill Beatson, Baltimore sportsman, and were staying in the houseboat George Bratt used to use while shooting canvasback during the ducking season. It was a nice layout and we arrived in the late afternoon in plenty of time to get all set for the early morning fishing.

Bill and I went in one boat and Frank and Frank Jr. used the other. We rowed back into the marsh and began to fish the shoreline. The water dropped off from 2 to 6 or 7 feet but there was enough shallow water where we wanted to fish. We used bugs and bass came slow. Finally Frank shouted across to us something about using another lure. I saw the flash of a spinner and knowing Frank, I told Bill to watch him start bringing in fish. Both Frank and his son are wizards with the spinner-fly combination, and at once they began to connect. Everytime they hit a fish they would give a war whoop, and whoops came fast and furious. They really went to town and when we met for lunch, they were way out in front of us.

That afternoon we both hit a point that had a long, shallow bar jutting out from it. The tide was pouring out and as we neared the place we saw bass working across the bar. Sometimes their backs came out of the water as

54

they swam across the shallows. It was quite a sight and we watched—for maybe a second! Then everyone was tossing lures in front of them. In that shallow water the strikes were hard and spectacular and we all took fish, but Frank gave a special exhibition of the use of his particular gear on the acrobatic bronzebacks. In one instance, when he was holding his rod high and bringing the lure back fast so as not to snag on the bottom, a bass chased the lure at least 15 feet before striking, and then churned the water and on one of his jumps almost landed on shore.

During the same trip I watched Frank using the fly-spinner combination in the thick grass. He would pick out a hole in the vegetation, drop the lure on the far side, let it sink a second, then bring it slowly along. I saw him take three bass that way and each one of them hit as the fly was about to be picked up for the next cast. Then the bass would either dive in the grass or double back through the hole and try for the other side. One of them hit, and when Frank struck, came out of the water. Keeping the pressure on, Frank skidded him over the grass into deeper water where he could play him more easily. It was spinner fishing at its best, and good to see.

Frank also had two streamer patterns that he used without a spinner—a yellow feathered fly with a red hackle, and a white feather job with red hackle. Both these flies were tied on 1/0 hooks, and largemouth seemed to love them. Tied with the long, saddle hackle feathers flaired outward, they had lots of action, as Frank retrieved them in slow, foot-long jerks.

Whatever the lure, just so it's a fly-rod one, brackish-water largemouth will usually co-operate. There are times when they are moody and times when you just can't bring a strike. But even then, you keep fishing because you never know when they are going to start and when they do start, you are in for a lot of real sport. They are generous hitters and good fighters and surely must have big hearts. They make you like them and give you so much enjoyment that before long you are putting them all back in the water unharmed for some other angler to have fun with, and just because they deserve to go back. A great game fish!

While there are many well-tried and established fly-rod lures for brackish-water largemouth black bass, it is also true that when they are in the mood, they will take a crack at practically anything you offer. Lure *play* seems more important than the lure itself. However, large bass do seem to like a big lure and extra large popping bugs have proved consistent takers of better-than-average-size bass. The Richmond bug accounted for many a bass over 6 pounds, all caught in brackish water, and the comparatively new Joe Brooks popper has done deadly damage to huge largemouth.

In streamers, those tied on 3/0 hooks and having feathers 4½ inches long, pay off in bigger fish than the smaller streamers and bucktails. The exception comes during the hot summer months when smaller lures seem to do better, but even then, in the early morning and at dusk, the larger lures come into their own again.

4.

Shad

The shad is a peculiar and somewhat mysterious cuss. He is an anadromous fish—one which ascends fresh-water streams to spawn—but instead of traveling coast-wise, as so many other species do, after the spawning season is over he performs a bathic migration. That is, he goes straight out to sea and disappears into the great depths beyond the continental shelf. Where he goes and what he does until springtime, no one knows any too well. But in the early spring he reappears at the mouths of bays and rivers and awaits the correct time to enter the estuaries and proceed on up to the spawning ground. For, as if to further establish his reputation as an unusual character, the shad does not spawn until the water has reached his exact, preferred temperature. Seldom does he enter a river until the water temperature is 50 degrees. Spawning occurs when the thermometer indicates about 60 degrees, and the eggs hatch in a week.

Because of the vagaries of the weather, therefore, the spawning date varies from year to year and from one coastal area to another. But generally speaking, on the east coast of the United States the shad begin their ascent of the rivers in Florida in January and at consecutively later dates as one proceeds northward. Usually it is June before they hit the fresh waters of the St. Lawrence watershed. They come up the rivers in waves of increasingly larger fish. Roe shad are the bigger ones, averaging about 6 pounds apiece. The smaller buck averages about 3½ pounds. On the Susquehanna River, the big latecomers are called, locally, "poplar backs." Some of these gals are scrappers, too, weighing as much as 8 pounds.

The natural range of the shad is from the St. John's River in Florida, up along the eastern seaboard to the St. Lawrence. Such rivers as the Potomac, the Connecticut, the Chickahominy, and the Susquehanna are all well-known fly-fishing waters for shad. But from Florida to Newfoundland, in most any fresh-water river that is accessible from the ocean, shad will be found and can be taken on fly-fishing equipment; provided several factors are right. There should be a current and usually the water should be shallow. However, if the current is swift enough, shad will hit in deep water such as is found immediately below a dam. The water should be clear as even slightly murky water will discourage them from striking the lure.

Shad were also introduced on the West Coast of the United States in 1871, with plantings of fry obtained from the Hudson River. Subsequent plantings have resulted in their becoming more plentiful along the Pacific Coast from San Diego, California, to Wrangel, Alaska. On the Pacific Coast, as far as can be learned, the first runs seem to hit the rivers successively, from south to north, during the months of May and June. Although a few sportsmen go out after shad every year in the Coos River, the Yaquina, the Columbia, and the Siuslaw, fly fishing for this species is still very much in its infancy in the West. However, I recently heard of two anglers who have been taking shad within the city limits of Portland, Oregon. Polly Rosborough, of Chiloquin, Oregon, has also sent me two shad flies which a friend of his invented and with which he has taken many fish. The fly is called the McCredie Special and certainly looks as if it has what it takes to bring strikes from shad.

Don Harger, of Salem, Oregon, well-known fly tier and editor of a fishing column in the *Oregon Statesman,* reports that huge quantities of shad are netted, frozen, and ground up as chum for tuna every year. A sport fisherman who knows the fighting quality of this game fish and the delicacy of shad and shad roe as a table item can only groan!

Its value as a food fish was probably the reason that ichthyologists started the artificial propagation of shad as far back as 1867. However, statistics show that even with artificial aid there has been a steady decline in their ranks. Overfishing commercially, and pollution of streams and bays, are no doubt among the causes of this depletion, but a major contributing factor is the erection of dams across rivers—dams that shut the shad off from their natural spawning beds and often leave the beds below the dams exposed for many hours. In the pool below the Conowingo Dam on the Susquehanna River, I have seen schools of hundreds of fish swimming around in large circles, wanting to go higher up the river to their natural spawning beds in the shallow water over the sand-and-gravel bottom. But the spawning urge must be satisfied, so they eventually disperse and scatter over the bars below the dam and spawn there. Just how great a loss there is under such conditions, no one knows. But on Sundays, at that point, during the summer months the turbines are turned off and practically the whole river bed is exposed. The loss from that one operation alone must be terrific.

And as one sees dams, either planned or already in the building, all over the country, one wonders whether a course in icthyology should not be enforced reading for an engineering degree. Certainly the policy of "To hell with the fish," as apparently followed by many dam builders, is one that future generations will deplore. While many such dams do not affect the various salt-water species, a few of the latter, such as shad, the steelhead, Atlantic salmon, and other anadromous fish are adversely influenced by any changes in the rivers which form their spawning beds, and sportsmen on both coasts should give wary reading to any plans to alter such rivers.

Although shad have been striking flies and small spoons and wobblers for many years and there are records of those fish being caught on flies in the Susquehanna River some seventy-five years ago, it was Tom Loving of Baltimore who really started modern fly fishing for the species. Twenty-seven years ago, while out after bass on the Susquehanna, he noticed several shad swimming in a shallow pool. As he watched, he saw one of them hit a silvery minnow. That night he tied a small white bucktail and could hardly wait till morning to get back to the river and try it. He caught shad at once and then, noticing the way the fish chewed his jaws up and down trying to dislodge the hook, he began to tie the fly on a double hook.

60

Personally, I don't like double hooks but Tom's lure took shad and with that fly he most certainly started the present-day popularity of fly fishing for shad.

Since then, fly casters have become increasingly aware of this sporty game fish that hits with a thud, takes to the air, fights hard and fast underneath the surface, and all in all, lets you know you've been in a battle before he comes to net.

The strike of shad to a fly is much like that of their distant cousin, the tarpon. They come up in a looping roll, take the fly and head down with it. They also have a disconcerting way of hitting the lure several times before they take. Once when I was fishing a fast glide of 2-foot deep water on the Susquehanna River, I ran bang into a school of shad making their way upstream. I anchored the rowboat and started casting. In that fast, shallow water they hit hard and did some fine and fancy jumping. They took line and lay broadside in the current, and really gave me a workout. Sometimes I would hook one within 10 feet of the boat, and when a big shad hits that close in you think he's going to pull you overboard. But the thing I remember best about that encounter was the way they would follow the fly and hit it several times before becoming hooked. That really shakes you!

It is unusual to run into such fast fishing as that, as shad are not customarily so eager for a fly when they are in schools. Most of the time the big roe shad pick out a resting place in a pool and from that position, much like the Atlantic salmon, rise up to take your offering. The largest number of shad that I know of being taken in one day in recent times, was seventeen. A good average for a full day of fishing would be five or six fish. Anglers who do not know the difference between true shad and hickory shad often report some staggering catches of the latter as "shad." The hickory is a ready fly taker and much more numerous, so that when a run of hickories hits a river, large numbers of them are caught.

One of the most memorable encounters I ever had with a fish of any kind took place when I hooked a shad in the Susquehanna River during the spring run of 1933. Fred Narvel, who was guiding me, rowed out to a pool below the Conowingo Dam and swung the boat so that I would be casting the lower part where the water shallowed and slowed somewhat before tipping over the lip. Tying on a OO drone, I started to cast in 45-foot throws and retrieve in foot-long jerks. On the tenth cast, as I started the retrieve, everything stopped dead! I pulled back with the rod but nothing gave.

"I'm on a rock, Fred," I said. "You had better drop back and let me get the lure off."

I stood there with rod held high, line tight, waiting for Fred to maneuver the boat so that I could free my hook. I glanced over my shoulder and there was Fred, smiling quietly and rowing slowly upstream. And at just about that moment, the rod was almost knocked from my hand and the reel started to scream. My rock had turned into a shad!

"What happened?" I asked Fred, as I settled into the fight.

"Well," he replied, "he hit and then swung broadside to the current until he decided that something was wrong. I was rowing upstream the entire time."

I gasped as the surface exploded and 5 pounds of shad plunged out and hung glistening in the sun. Then he was back in the water, bulldogging it across current while I prayed that my 6-pound test leader would hold. He took line and I hung on as best I could. Then he shot out again in a graceful, looping leap. A moment later he decided to come upstream and I had to strip line frantically as he bored into the flow of the current. Then he swirled on top, reversed his field, and slipped downstream, tearing line off the reel but fast! He turned on the surface, showing his broad, deep side. That took more line but at last he stopped and lay doggo, resting.

I started to pump, then, and that made him decide to swim upstream. I kept the pressure on and gradually worked him in close to the boat.

"Get your net, Fred," I shouted. "I'll swing him in."

"He's not ready yet," Fred answered, and at the same moment I noticed that my rod tip was bent almost double.

I tried to take the strain off so fast that I gave him slack. He gained twenty yards on that play but this time I started him back and kept him coming until Fred slipped the net under him and brought him in to the boat.

"A rock, eh?" commented Fred, holding the fish up. "He'll go about 6 pounds. I mean *she* will. She's a roe fish."

I felt weak and shaky. "Boy, oh boy!" I gasped. "Those babies really can fight."

"Took twenty minutes," Fred answered.

Part of the fun of fly-fishing for shad lies in the fact that in different rivers the species seems to prefer different lures. Unlike most other salt-water fish, which will hit pretty much the same lures even when found 3000 miles apart, old *Alosa sapidissima* likes his menu varied to suit his location. Where the Susquehanna flows into the Chesapeake Bay in Maryland, they favor the OO drone, while far up in Nova Scotia, Canada, believe it or not, the shad will lambaste the feathers out of an Atlantic salmon fly.

Sifford Pearre of Baltimore, who has been fishing the Susquehanna for years, knew, as we all did that the OO Huntington Drone or the OO Metalure was by far the best dish for our local shad. So one summer when, during a visit to Nova Scotia, Sifford found the nearby river full of fresh-run shad, he dug deep into his tackle box until he found a single lonely OO drone. He tied it on, hastened to the river, and began to cast. He cast and cast over shad that scorned his drone completely, not even deigning to wiggle a fin at it. At last the disgusted angler reached into his fishing vest, pulled out his Atlantic salmon flies, and tied on a size 8 silver doctor. His first cast brought a strike and from then on he had some of the best shad fishing in all his experience. They hit silver doctors, silver grays, mar lodge, and Jock Scotts. Feverishly Sifford went through his fly box, putting on different patterns of salmon flies. They hit them all and wanted more.

The next spring found Sifford on the Susquehanna, all ready to confound Maryland anglers with his discovery. But two days of futile casting of Atlantic salmon flies brought not a single strike. Out came the OO drone and the shad began to hit. Whatever the cause, salmon flies worked in the northern waters but didn't have what it takes on the Susquehanna. The drone was good on the

Chickahominy and the Potomac, too, while salmon flies have failed everywhere except in Nova Scotia.

On the Connecticut River a OO drone will take shad, all right, but a sparsely tied fly is best, and particularly well liked is one which is comprised of a red bead ahead of the eye of the hook, then mostly bare hook with just ⅛ inch of feather dyed orange or red sticking up from the back.

On the West Coast, shad like a small silver spoon, a small white bucktail, and a silver spinner-white bucktail combination.

Fishing for shad always reminds me a little of salmon fishing; once they start upstream they seem to frequent the same type of water. Upon entering the rivers they spread out and often stay for lengthy periods in pools down river before heading for the spawning grounds. At this time they move about to a limited extent and offer good targets for fly fishermen. A favorite place to cast is at the tails of the pools, where the shad lie during the daytime. As dusk nears, they drift out to the heads of the pools, preparatory to moving upstream. The shore line also offers productive spots for a well-placed lure, as shad will often follow the shore as they travel upriver. Glides and fast runs pay, too, just as in salmon or trout fishing.

During the period when they are going upriver, shad do not school to any extent, but go in pairs or threesomes —usually a big roe shad followed by a couple of smaller bucks. The bucks stay close to the object of their affections and will follow a hooked roe all the way into the boat. You will often see a roe shad near the spawning act, flanked by bucks pressing against her sides as they swim along. And on one occasion, while fishing the Chicka-hominy with Monk Montague, not once, but twice, in netting fish we came up with both the hooked roe and a free-swimming buck. That same trip also gave us a perfect illustration of how shad will follow a current in their journey upstream. We were fishing the river 25 miles be-low Richmond, Virginia, and the water was 30 feet deep where we were stationed, immediately below the dam. Yet the migrating fish stayed close to the surface as they moved along and almost every cast into the current brought a strike.

In casting to shad, it is best to throw across the river, wait fifteen or twenty seconds after the lure hits the sur-face for it to sink, then retrieve it in foot-long jerks. Con-ditions being right—fairly warm water and not too much of it—you will do business, providing the fish are there. When the water is cold, they go deep and just don't rise to a fly or a spoon.

At the times when the shad enter the rivers, there is usually plenty of water coming down and this adds to the problem of getting a lure down to deep-lying fish. That's when the OO drone is at its best. Cast up current so that the drone will sink as it floats downstream, then when you start your retrieve there is some chance of a fish seeing and rising to it.

Once hooked, the shad brings out a wide selection of tricky ways of trying to escape, one of the most notable being his habit of champing the hook. The shad has a thin cheek and the hook often pulls down through it, making a tear that will sometimes allow the hook to work

66

out. The chewing action hastens the tearing of the cheek and aids the fish to dislodge and throw the lure. A tight line is the only defense and that doesn't always work. I have seen a shad still methodically grinding his jaws as he was being netted, and have lost more than one fish which literally chewed its way free of the hook.

Shad will hit small bucktails and spinner-bucktail combinations now and then. They hit the small, scantily tied Connecticut shad fly hard and often. But for consistent strikes, no other lure seems to have the same appeal for shad as does the OO Huntington Drone and the metalure and trix-oreno. Shad definitely go for spoon-type lures.

Allow the lure to sink a foot or two before starting the retrieve, and then, when brought back in slow, foot-long jerks, these spoon-type foolers have what it takes to set shad on the prod.

5.

Hickory Shad

The hickory shad, *Pomolobus mediocris*, reaches a top weight of 3 pounds and like his cousin, the shad proper, is sought by fly casters all along the Atlantic Coast. He uses most of the same waters as shad and differs in habit only in that he will leave the main river and ascend smaller tributary streams in which to perform the propagation act. There is one sure-fire way to identify these two very similar species: when closed, the mandibles of the shad come together evenly, while in the hickory shad the lower mandible juts out beyond the upper.

Unlike the shad, however, the hickory is not a table fish, although some anglers extract the roe from the female. But for pure sport, hickory shad should not be overlooked by fly-fishermen. They are numerous and when the run is in, they are willing strikers to an artificial lure and are plenty of fun after they are on. They hit hard with a slash that you feel right down into the rod butt. They often slap the lure several times before you hook them, which makes it a good idea to continue the retrieve until the lure is in close to the boat.

The same technique recommended for shad applies to

the hickory. Cast across current, let the fly sink a foot, then bring it back in foot-long jerks, not too fast. In small streams, some anglers prefer to cast their fly across current, and let it swing down and through until it comes to a stop below them. Hickories usually take a fly played in that manner just as it has completed the downward drift and starts the swing in toward shore. This way of presenting the fly takes fish, but after years of trying every kind of retrieve and catching many hundreds of hickories, I have found that the best retrieve, regardless of the fly or lure used, is that which I recommend above.

Once hooked, the hickory does a lot of jumping and wages a strong fight for a while. Then his habit of swimming up against the current allows you to bring your catch in in a hurry. Regardless of that one trait, the hickory is a very nice fly-rod fish.

In the Chickahominy and also the Potomac and the Susquehanna, they come up the river in waves, the first fish usually being smaller and the size increasing with each run, until the last wave brings the 3-pound fish.

Usually they hit best in shallow water as they follow the glides and fast runs. The head of a pool in the fast water is always a good place for them. There are exceptions, of course, and sometimes they like to take it easy in the deeper parts of the pools. One day when we had heard that the hickories were in the Patuxent River in Maryland, Chet Bedell, Pete Chambliss, and I drove down for our first try for them on that river. We fished in the neighborhood of Upper Marlboro where the Patuxent is more like a trout stream than the big river it becomes down toward the Chesapeake Bay. There are swift runs

70

and fairly deep pools. Branches of trees hanging down to the water's edge put a hazard in casting and the occasional narrowing or widening of the river forms interesting pools and ripples.

Things went slow for a while, then Chet took three in a row and Pete came through with a couple. I took one and lost one and then started figuring things out. The fast ripples didn't seem to hold anything and that meant the fish were not moving upstream. Therefore, they had to be in the pools, and from the way those we had caught had acted, they had to be in the deepest parts of the pools, just resting there and not moving around at all. I went upstream from my companions and scouted for deep pools. When I had found one that looked to have what I wanted, I took off the small white bucktail I had been using and put on a OO drone. Casting out, I let the drone sink until I feared losing it on obstructions on the bottom, then started it back in a very slow retrieve, not trying to make it spin but endeavoring to impart a lazy wobble to it.

Things happened! I took eight fish in a row, and by that time Pete and Chet were coming upstream double quick. They had seen me fighting fish and wanted in. I explained my method to them and each went off, searching for the deep pools. From then on, we all took fish in that manner.

On another hickory-fishing trip I was fishing with Jack Nelson, of Washington, on the Potomac River just above Chain Bridge and having a very thin time of it. We cast and retrieved our spoons in the regular manner with never a strike. At the point where we were fishing, the river narrows and deepens and the main current rushes through with plenty of power. The deal is to stand on the rocks, cast out into the current, allow the lure to sink, then bring it back through the eddies between the current and the rocks—water which was 10 feet deep, but still the only place you could get any action.

Generally when they were hitting they were up near the top, but this day they just wouldn't co-operate. Yet we knew they were in because we saw jiggers at work, jiggers being guys who attach a gang hook to a stout line, tie the line to a stiff pole, then drop the hooks into the water and work them up and down until they snag some unsuspecting hickory that happens to be swimming by. We talked it over and decided that the fish were deep. So we tied some "wraparound" lead on our leaders and went to work. We would cast out, let the drone sink deep, then bring it back in a slow retrieve. At once we took fish. Some would hit deep, some half way up, and some followed the lure to the surface before striking.

We landed them, took them off the hook, and returned them to the water, while the jigging boys looked at us as if we were crazy. We must have landed seventy-five within a couple of hours. We had great fun catching them but still more fun watching the expression on the faces of the jiggers.

Again emulating his cousin the shad, the hickory has a specialized taste in lures and I've seen them turn up their noses at one lure and ten seconds later slap the daylights out of another one. Burt Dillon, of Baltimore, invented a fly called simply "Dillon's Shad Fly" and with it he has taken many hickories—and shad, too. But hickories really go for it and that fly takes them when others go blank. The first time I saw it in action was on a trip Burt and I took to the Octororo Creek, which empties into the Susquehanna River about a mile below the Conowingo Dam. Burt had told me that the Octororo was loaded with hickories and it didn't take long to find out that the statement was true. Rather, I should say, it didn't take long for Burt to show me. He used the Dillon Shad Fly and started to catch fish at once. Where we were fishing the bushes came down to the water's edge, and since there was no room for a backcast, we had to roll cast. I had a drone on, at first, but that didn't last long because trying to roll out a drone is like trying to cast a rock tied to the end of a 4X leader. Then I put on a small bucktail and business picked up. But Burt was having action almost every cast and I began wishing for one of his flies. Finally I couldn't stand it any longer.

"Is that the only Dillon fly you have?" I asked.

Burt grinned and handed one over to me. "As a matter of fact," he said, "I only brought two with me, so take good care of that one."

That fly really had something. Hickories went for it like Brooklyn fans for "dem bums." We pounded them so hard that they finally went down and we had to move on to another pool.

Since there were so many fish in the river, I figured that this would be a good time to try a bit of experimenting. I knew that hickory shad liked small lures and felt that a small hook was far better than a large one. So when we started on the next pool, I took off the Dillon Shad Fly and put on a white bucktail about 2 inches long and tied on a 1/0 hook. I fished it hard but nothing came of it, while Burt took fish after fish with his fly. Then I switched to a smaller lure and had a couple of halfhearted strikes. Finally I put on a drone and started catching fish, but still took far less than Burt did. So back on went the Dillon Fly and action started immediately. Fish came on almost every cast and becoming careless, I lifted one up by the leader when I was landing him. The 4-pound test tippet snapped, the hickory fell back into the water, and away went the Dillon fly.

I looked up to see Burt scowling at me. "That was my last fly," he said, "and you had to act careless like that."

He was retrieving his own fly and when he spoke to me he stopped his strip. Then, having finished telling me off, he started to bring the fly in. His rod dipped and stayed down. I started edging off downstream. Maybe he would get that fly free from the bottom and maybe he wouldn't, and if he didn't, I wanted to be far, far away. The only consolation was that it was time to go home anyway, and besides, strange as it may seem, we had both taken so many fish that we were getting tired of it.

The same lures that produce for the shad are the preferred menu of the hickory shad. Shiny, flashy, spoon-type lures do the trick and those favorites, the OO Huntington Drone, the metalure, and the trix-oreno are away out in front as strike producers.

Use the same tactics on the retrieve as you do for shad, too. Allow the lure to sink a foot or so, bring it back in slow, foot-long jerks and leave the rest to the willing hickories.

74

6.

Striped Bass

At Coos Bay, Oregon, in what seemed the shortest two hours I have ever spent fishing, I had two of the hardest, most vicious strikes I've ever experienced on a popping bug, and emerged from the fray with what proved to be the largest striped bass ever taken on a fly. Joe Bates and I were en route to the Klamath River in California, to have a go at steelhead. At Salem, Oregon, we stopped to pick up Don Harger and Chan Brown, and knowing my liking for stripers, they suggested that the party stop off at Coos Bay for an afternoon's fishing. We drove to Roy Self's dock, picked up Jimmie Christensen to guide us, and cruised out into the Bay looking for school fish breaking on top. Jimmie said there were plenty of schools of fish from 3 to 20 pounds around. But that day the surface was free of feeders, which was all right with me because I wanted big bull stripers, not the usually smaller school fish. I had just spotted the breakwater of the local airport and it looked like the place for bulls.

We eased in to look at the depth of the water along the breakwater and discovered that it was from 3 to 5 feet deep, out as far as 10 feet from the rocks. It was the kind of water that big stripers like. While the guide maneuvered the boat to a distance of about 60 feet off-shore, I put up my outfit, tapered the nylon leader down to a 12-pound test, and tied on a big white popping bug, which Bill Upperman of Atlantic City had made to my specifications.

I mounted the bow and started casting. I put the popper into the bank and let it lie there for a few seconds, then gave it a hard pop that threw water high, and let it rest a while. Then I popped it out slowly, picked it up, and cast again. The tide was coming in and was about three-quarters full and I knew from experience that it was the right stage of the water for good results. Ten minutes later, when I had played the bug out on a cast, and was about to lift it from the water, a tremendous swirl right under it almost made me strike. I managed somehow to let the bug sit there, then gave it a slight twitch. Again that terrific swirl lifted water and bug several inches. Again I managed to refrain from striking and let it lie still. After a bit, I gave it another pop and watched wide-eyed as that great boil of water appeared beneath it. I gulped, and started popping the bug in short jerks. Suddenly the water around it seemed to burst wide open. I struck, and it felt like trying to drive a needle into the side of the *Queen Mary*. I caught a flashing glimpse of the fish as he headed for deep water and I hung on with both hands as the reel screamed and the rod dipped violently and stayed down.

On he went, a fast run, full of power of a really big fish. I struggled to lift the rod as he whipped the line off the reel—200, 300, 400 feet. I looked at the backing, praying there was plenty left on the reel and was scared to find it mighty thin looking. Desperately I tightened and felt him slow, then pulled back on the rod and gradually stopped him. He hung out there for a minute before I started to get line back, then forced me to reel frantically as he swam my way. Things went well for a spell and then he wanted out again. Off he went, headed west in a hell of a hurry. This time he stopped after a mere 100 feet and once again I had him coming my way. When he was within 50 feet of the boat, he swirled on top. His dorsal fin stuck out and I gasped as I saw the outline of his body through the water. He was enormous.

Evidently he didn't like it up there, for after that one swirl he sounded, going deep and making me pump hard to lift him up again. This time he surfaced broadside to us. I gave him all the pressure I dared as I worked him in close. Then he spied the boat and did a fade out. I got him back in a hurry this time, roughed him in beside the boat and held him there while Jimmie gaffed and lifted him aboard.

"Forty minutes," I dimly heard someone say.

Later, when we weighed that striper, he tipped the scales at 29 pounds, 6 ounces. He was 42½ inches long and 25½ inches in girth.

That experience was the climax of many years of fly fishing for *roccus saxatilis*, the striped bass.

A willing taker of artificial lures wherever he is found, the striper is a push over for fly-rod foolers. He goes his way in water shallow enough that it is easy to put a fly within his line of vision and you can be reasonably certain, sea-going trencherman that he is, that is likely to come at it with open mouth. In addition, with a range covering thousands of miles of coastal water in both Pacific and Atlantic Oceans, he is accessible to thousands of fly casters.

Although the species was originally restricted to the East Coast, the habitat of the striped bass was considerably widened in 1879, when the state of California and the United States Government planted them in California waters in the vicinity of Monterey. Since that first planting, so many years ago, the striper has steadily pushed his way northward along the coast until now he is found in great numbers around Coos Bay, Oregon, and has been caught as far north as the Umpqua River in that same state. The weight of the western fish compares very favorably with those native to the Atlantic Coast, and the fact that West Coast striped bass are listed as game fish in California waters has helped considerably to swell the numbers in the Pacific Coast area.

On the Atlantic seaboard the fact that the striper is a spring spawner, and very prolific, offsets to some degree the strain put upon it by commercial fishermen. Along the East Coast, the stripers range from the St. John's River in northern Florida to the Gulf of St. Lawrence. They reach their greatest concentration in that area from Cape Cod to perhaps the central portion of North Carolina. Some of the favorite fishing spots are off Cuttyhunk and Martha's Vineyard, Massachusetts, in Rhode Island, Connecticut, Barnegat Inlet, New Jersey, and in the Chesapeake Bay. Along the coasts of all the middle Atlantic states they are found in the surf and along jetties, as well as in the bays and estuaries and rivers leading into the ocean.

Striped bass go into bays and rivers to spawn and often ascend the rivers some distance, feeding voraciously on the herring which have come upstream for the same purpose. They stay in the rivers until the water chills in the fall, at which time they go back to the bays and the ocean and lie in deep holes where the temperature is more constant during the cold weather.

Stripers reach great weights. There is a record of one weighing 125 pounds, taken in nets at Edenton, North Carolina, but the official world top weight for striped bass is 73 pounds. This fish was taken on hook and line in Vineyard Sound, Massachusetts, in 1913. The larger stripers are not confined to the ocean, as might be believed, and many huge stripers have been taken in bays, estuaries, and rivers. It has been my experience that the big bull stripers like to cruise such waters as Chesapeake Bay and Coos Bay, where there are numerous breakwaters, bars, and other shallow places—which very circumstance puts them at the mercy of a well-placed bucktail or popping bug.

Like every other fish, stripers have certain peculiarities that may be related to one or another area where they are found. Bill Upperman, of Atlantic City, says that in the spring the stripers get cataracts on their eyes, and as a result are for a while impervious to artificial lures. He says that at this time he has seen huge schools of them feeding with heads down and tails up, searching their food out by scent alone.

While relatively unknown to many a present-day sport fisherman, fly fishing for striped bass is by no means a new development. Along the Atlantic Coast a scattered handful of fly casters have been having the time of their lives for the past twenty-five years, taking striped bass on large white streamers and bucktails. But only during the last few years have great numbers of anglers taken to the salt with the light rod and discovered the joys of fly fishing for stripers.

Once you have caught a striper on a bucktail or popping bug, you become a dyed-in-the-wool striped-bass addict. It does things to you that you don't forget and when you know it's time for them to be cruising, you just can't stay away from their hangouts.

Most fly-fishing for stripers is done from a boat, as it is easier to get to them that way than by wading or fishing from the shore. Skiffs or rowboats are quite suitable, either with or without outboard motor; a cruiser or charter boat is the deal when going farther afield. The captain will know, in the latter case, whether it is advisable to tow a skiff or whether it is possible to fish directly from the cruiser.

As I have said, big stripers like shallow water. They cruise the beaches in the surf. They loaf around jetties and inlets and are found feeding along the banks in bays and estuaries. They like bars and rocky points. They like to stick close to the overhanging banks of shallow bays in water from 2 to 5 feet deep and rush out to engulf a choice bit of food. They will work breakwaters and bridges and any other obstruction in the water.

I call the big fish that range these shallow waters "bull stripers." They go from 20 pounds up, and their vicious wallop to a popping bug is one of the most startling things in all my fishing experience. With such big stripers

80

it is advisable to use a big lure. The larger the fly, the more interested the striper will be, and the same small fly that might play havoc with school fish leaves the big boys cold. They don't even bother to look at it. It is quite possible to take large numbers of stripers from 2 to 10 pounds on a fly 2 inches long. But you could cast your arm off before you would get a 15-pound fish to look at the same fly.

This was brought home to me very vividly on the occasion of a trip to Martha's Vineyard. I was fishing with Hal Lyman and Reggie Ellis on Captain Joe Eldridge's boat, appropriately named *Striper*. We cruised slowly along the shallow, rock-infested water immediately under the varicolored cliffs of Gay Head. It was great striper water.

Hal and Reggie were using light surf-casting rods and large popping plugs. Unfortunately, I had come away without a single big bucktail or popper and was restricted to black-bass flies and black-bass poppers. There was no doubt the fish were there, because I watched Reggie and Hal each land a 23-pounder, and I had two follows, well behind my small lures, and saw one or two halfhearted swirls nearby. But in all that good water, not a single strike did I have to those small lures.

Tidal action controls the stay of the big stripers in these shallow places and the best time to find them in their favorite feeding grounds is from halfway up on the incoming tide to halfway down on the outgoing. On a dropping tide, they like to move out to deeper water.

When fishing a popping bug to these big boys, it is wise to play it slowly. Drop it on the surface and let it

81

sit there for half a minute before giving it a hard pop— the harder the better. Jerk it hard enough to throw the water a foot in the air, then let it sit motionless for ten or fifteen seconds before giving it another hard pop. Then bring it in in a series of short pops. Keep casting to the edge of the place to which you are fishing. Extra long casts are not necessary. A throw of 35 to 50 feet should be plenty long enough, and if the fish are there and you persist, you will be in for fireworks.

I don't know of any fishing that is harder on the nerves than using a popping bug for bull stripers. Every moment you expect the bottom of the bay to do a Vesuvius and when it does, it still catches you unaware. The striper doesn't just raise up and sock the bug—he has a maddening way of swirling under it several times, and each time the water seems to be raised up several inches. After a couple of such maneuvers, the angler is nearly crazy. He wants to shout, he has to keep the bug coming, and he must rest it at the proper times. The water is boiling, and every second he is expecting that smashing hit. It's hell, but, oh boy!

Once the bull striper hits, he dashes off on a dazzling run of 300 or 400 feet. Sometimes they dive at the end of the run and if there are any obstructions under the water, you can be pretty sure it will be curtains. But if you are able to pump them up after that first plunge toward the bottom, they seldom go deep again. Generally they stay on top, broadside to the boat, where they swirl and fight away from you, sometimes with the dorsal fin right out of water. It's a great sight to watch a 20-pound fish put up such a fight.

Below the Conowingo Dam on the Susquehanna River, there are 4 miles of fresh water before you hit the salt. Stripers come in there to spawn, usually during late March, and stay until the cold water chases them out in November. It is not unusual to hang onto 25- and 30-pounders.

Some years ago I fished that stretch with Fred Narvel and his son Charlie. They had never seen a striper taken on a fly and that day I had the pleasure of being with Charlie when he saw his first striper perform in the manner I have been describing. We were fishing a pool about 2 miles below the dam and my third cast brought a 5-pounder charging in. He hit hard and fast, and remembering my stories about how a bull swirls first, Charlie said, "I didn't see any big swirls that time."

"That's just a baby," I replied. "Wait until a 20-pounder gets under it."

Small fish seemed to be everywhere that day and they kept socking away at the popper. But although they put up some scrappy fights, there was no sign of the big one I was looking for.

I had to be home early, and time was running out as we rowed over to a pool near the shore. The water was about 8 feet deep and it looked good to me. I cast and recast, for fifteen minutes, without a sign of life. Then it happened. The water bulged up under the bug, and behind me I heard Charlie gasp. I wanted to see his face but didn't dare to look away from the water, as I popped the bug again. Then, realizing that the lure was much nearer the boat than it should have been, I looked back. Charlie was sitting there transfixed, quite unmindful of the fact that the current was carrying the boat right over the pool where our fish was. In answer to my shout, he snapped out of his trance and rowed out of the pool and anchored.

"I sure never saw anything like that before!" he said.

We rested the fish for about fifteen minutes, and then I began to cast again. This time he came up in a hurry. His nose hit the bug and knocked it a couple of inches in the air. It was too much for my nerves at that moment, and I struck—and, of course, missed. But I had the bug back to him in a jiffy. I popped it, and a big swirl came up.

"He swirled deep that time," I said. Then I popped the lure again and this time he came closer to the surface. The water moved up and the bug shimmied on top of it.

"Keep our position, Charlie," I started. "He's going to—"

And then he hit! He went down river like a torpedo and even though we let the boat drift after him, he had my reel almost cleared of backing before I could stop him. We kept drifting down and eventually I began to get line back. Then gradually I began to move him upstream. Forty-five minutes later, and almost a mile below where he struck, he was in the boat, 16½ pounds of fighting beauty.

Charlie's sufficient comment was, "Now I know what you mean."

Charlie was also in on one of the most exciting bits of striper fishing I've ever had the pleasure of watching. "B" Goodwin, of Baltimore, was fishing the Susquehanna, with Charlie acting as guide, in June of 1949. I was along in another boat with Fred Narvel, and we sat in on a bit of fast and furious action that was so exciting that we stopped fishing to watch the show. It all started when Charlie rowed B up to a pool and B made his first cast into it. A hard strike came at once but the fish missed the big white Upperman popping bug. B cast right back to him and this time he took hard and fought through the fast water on the edge of the pool—a 5-pounder. The next cast brought another strike and this time B wound up with a 3-pounder. That's when Fred and I stopped fishing and rowed over to see what was happening. B's next cast brought another strike and then I saw him turn and speak to Charlie. The latter, who had been holding the boat still against the current, rowed upstream a way, dropped anchor, and paid out line until the boat was back in its former position. Then I saw him reach down and come up with a fly rod. He put on a white popper and then he too started casting. Right away he began to catch fish and between the two of them they seemed to have fish on all the time. They really were working at it and from where we were it was plenty nice to watch the bugs popping hard along the surface and see the water fly as the fish hit. That flurry lasted for about half an hour before the fish stopped hitting. In that time they had landed ten fish from 3 to 10 pounds and had, I guess, thirty strikes.

Stripers like that big white popping bug, and I think part of the allure of the bug is the fact that it is made of balsa wood. In addition to giving a good loud pop and throwing lots of water, it has lightness and buoyancy enough to make it seem alive as you work it. It skips and skids along the surface and when you give it a long, hard strip, it shoots through the water causing all sorts of commotion. Stripers hit that bug when they are turning up their noses at other lures. It casts very well indeed, and has the necessary size to interest big fish.

Once in a while you tie into a sulker. He will hit the bug and immediately go deep. There he does his stuff, swimming slowly along or lying doggo and refusing to come up no matter how hard you pump. And though eventually you will get him to the surface, he will usually go down again and once more you will grow arm-weary as you try to raise him.

The second strike mentioned in the opening lines of this chapter, on the occasion of my trip to Coos Bay, Oregon, was from such a fish. I had boated the 29½-pounder and started to cast again, and almost immediately I saw that typical swirl of a big fish. I waited until the water subsided and then gave the bug a hard pop. It missed the pop, however, and skittered madly across the surface. And just as it stopped skittering and I was going to lift it out of the water, Mr. Striper came out in a looping smash. I almost lost the rod as he hit with all the power of his heavy body in back of him, but I gave him the works.

It rocked me to the heels, and then he was off along the surface on a careening run that sent water flying in all directions. The reel sang and the air rang with shouts of advice and encouragement from the boys. But after only a 200-foot run, that striper went down deep and sat there and sulked. I hit the rod butt with the heel of my hand. I leaned back hard and gave the tackle everything it would take. I did everything I could think of to raise that boy, but I couldn't budge him. Instead of coming up, he just bore off, slow and steady, tugging all the time to go even deeper. It took half an hour of grueling work to get that bird to the top. Then he showed close to the boat and I realized with thumping heart that he was at least as big and perhaps even a little bigger than the first one! But I'll never know—for he stayed on top for a moment, then dove, and as he went down the popper pulled out and came bobbing to the top.

While popping bugs seem to be the best lure for big stripers in shallow water, the large white bucktail performs better where there is wave action. Breakers and whitecaps stir the water up so much that they prevent the fish from seeing the action of a surface lure and in such conditions it is better to go down deep with a bucktail.

At Barnegat Inlet I had an opportunity, not long ago, to confirm this belief. Barnegat is one of the great concentration spots for stripers on the Atlantic Coast. They stay there in goodly numbers most of the year and in the fall some of the larger fish move in and furnish a little extra fun until late November, when the colder water sends them out to the deep.

I was fishing with Monk Montague of Richmond, Virginia, and we were guided by Captain Andy Bjornberg. On his boat, the *Queen o' Hearts,* we headed into water that was ideal for stripers. There were rocks, jetties, and breakers, with the added hazard for us of numerous pilings along the jetty, sticking up some distance above the water. These pilings were encrusted with barnacles and when a striper manages to run your leader across one of them, it usually cuts it.

Andy eased the *Queen* into the white water and Monk

made his first cast with a bucktail and was immediately hooked into a 5-pounder. My white popper didn't bring a strike. It continued to go unnoticed until we hit the quieter water beyond the breakers. Then, as the bug lay still on the surface, a 7-pounder rolled up and swallowed it. And from there, right to the end of the jetty, although Monk took a couple of fish on the bucktail, I had the bulk of the action. We headed back, then, and on this run I used a bucktail, too, and as we neared the surf, we both took fish. On the next journey seaward we both changed to poppers. This time we took an equal number of fish on each rod.

We had started to fish at daylight and when we stopped at nine A.M., we had taken thirty-four stripers, up to 12 pounds, and had more than verified our opinions as to the use of the two popular lures.

Fishing into jetties such as those at Barnegat, where the rocks protrude several feet at low tide and lie a foot or so beneath the surface when the tide is high, is adventurous angling. At Barnegat, the captain cruises as slowly as possible along the rocks and pilings, holding the boat as steady as he can in the swirl of eddies and the crash of breakers. But as the waves pour through the inlet, the 30-foot cruiser is often knocked 6 feet sideways, on the turn, and under these conditions casting can be a bit of a job. You must maintain your balance and still manage to put that lure in against the rocks where the stripers like to lie and wait for food to be washed over to them. Sometimes when the popping bug or bucktail is tossed to them, they grab it and dash across the rocks to do their fighting from the other side. This may mean a cut leader and there is nothing to be done about it but accept the loss—small payment, after all, for the fun you will have with those that stay on your side of the fence.

It's surprising though, how those nylon leaders take the rough-and-tumble fishing at Barnegat. On one of my first trips there, I hooked a fish that tore across the rocks, veered off to the left, and ran 50 feet before I could stop him. He felt heavy and I leaned back on the rod hard, trying to get him started my way and back across the rocks again. I didn't have much luck, and Morrie Upperman, who was along, shouted, "You've really got a big one, this time."

The fish fought stubbornly and I only brought him back by inches, and all the while my leader was working across one of the barnacle-encrusted piles that stick up from the rocks. Finally he came over the barrier and I landed him— a 12-pounder. Then I looked at my leader. It was frayed over the entire length and the 12-pound test tippet looked like it was ready to disintegrate at any moment. I don't know how much longer it would have lasted, but I was glad the fish was in the boat.

Always, when fishing for stripers, it pays to keep an eye out for school fish. Sometimes you will see them hitting at bait. Then you can quite often take one or two fish before the school moves out of range. Keeping up with them is something of a problem but frequently when you do lose them, you can locate them again by watching the movement of gulls, which follow the schools. Sometimes you will see flocks of gulls wheeling and diving over the water as they gather in the scraps left as the stripers cut into a school of bait fish. In fact, gull watching is part and parcel of striper fishing, as the birds seem to sense the presence of food even when they are miles away and you will see them heading for the free lunch from all directions.

School fish are setups for a bucktail. Most of the time they will strike the lure as often as it is put in front of them and the only problem for the angler is to keep up with their rapid movement and to relocate them after they have sounded and come up on a different tack. When a school does sound and seems lost entirely, it is always wise to wait for some time. On one occasion, as I was fishing a school of stripers in shallow water, they sounded. I turned off the outboard motor and just sat there waiting for them to come up. After a few minutes, out of the corner of my eye I saw a swirl close by. Instead of getting my fly in at once, I waited, and sure enough, there was another swirl about 30 feet away and this time I saw a flash of silver. I dropped the fly a couple of feet to the side of where the swirl had occurred and had hardly started the retrieve when a 3-pounder hit. And yet, if I had not been sitting there quietly watching for the fish, I would have thought they had kept on their way and had given me the slip.

Morley Griswold, well-known western steelhead angler and former governor of Nevada, fishes for stripers at Coos Bay, Oregon. He ties his own flies and consistently takes 20-pounders from the schools that work into the bay. He fishes with Ray Self out of the Sportsmen's Dock, in a small cruiser, the boat hanging off from the breaking school while Griswold casts. He has made some astounding catches. He usually starts his fishing about the fifteenth of September, at which time the big schools move into the bay. A couple of weeks later, and until the water becomes too cold and drives the fish to the deep, seems to be the best time to fish the shallow flats and breakwaters for the big bull stripers.

Since there is generally a fairly stiff breeze blowing in the bay, it is easier to fish from a cruiser than a small boat. Two men can cast at the same time. Don't forget a long-handled net or gaff for landing the fish.

Stripers hit a bucktail with a terrific smash. They take one so hard and fast that you can do nothing to stop that initial dash. You just hang on and let the drag on the reel help you. And as far as the retrieve of the bucktail is concerned, there seems to be no special technique required. I usually bring the lure back in slow, foot-long jerks, especially when fishing around jetties and breakwaters. Schoolfish fall for a faster, more even retrieve, comparatively speaking, than the bull striper, which seems to definitely like the foot-long jerk imparted to the lure.

In the early fall, too, when the stripers move into the shallow parts of bays and estuaries, they seem more willing to co-operate and hit the lure with a bang. But in water that thin—from 2 to 6 feet deep—care is necessary so as not to scare them. This is especially true where there are not any deep holes to which they could swim for safety. Under such circumstances, the lure should be fished slowly and with less noise than usual.

And always, when striper fishing, remember that sometimes you may see them rolling and often you will see them making swirls as they feed, although many a fish is taken from water that shows no signs of life. It pays to give every likely looking spot a thorough going over. Take it easy and throw back to the same place several times before moving along. It has become my creed to believe they are there, and to work carefully—and because of that belief I take some nice fish from apparently barren water.

The two best fly-rod lures for stripers seem to be the large popper tied on a 3/0 Z nickle hook and called the "Joe Brooks Popper," and the large white bucktail, also tied on a 3/0 Z nickle hook. Running those two a close race is the Joe Brooks Streamer Fly # 108, also tied on the 3/0 hook.

The main thing to remember in choosing a lure for stripers is that big stripers like big lures. Small lures just will not take large bass, and if fly rods were capable of throwing even larger lures than the ones mentioned above, I have no doubt that fly-rod anglers would catch even bigger fish.

7.

Bonefish

Albula vulpes, the bonefish, ranks with the world's top game fish. You do a bit of stalking as you search for him, call on all your casting ability as you put your fly to him, and require every bit of fish-playing experience on the books when he starts off on that sizzling, headlong dash for the deep.

The sight of a bonefish tail waving slowly above the surface of the shallow water where he customarily feeds does all kinds of things to you. You shiver and shake and tingle all over and your mouth goes dry. It is one of the great moments of all fishing experience, and the thrill of seeing his first tailing fish has turned many an expert into a tyro. It is a thrill that does not diminish with time, and after many months of persistent pursuit of the bonefish, I still go through those same symptoms of fever everytime I get ready to cast to a tailing fish.

Bonefish can *cure* a fever, too, as I learned first hand in the spring of 1948. I was on my way down to the Keys, in company with Monk Montague of Richmond. We stopped at Melbourne to say hello to Dick Splaine and found him down with a 101-degree fever. There was a flush on his face and a glassy look about his eyes.

"Poor guy!" we sympathized. "Here you are, sick, and we were going to ask you to go bonefishing with us."

"Sure will!" said Dick, sitting up in bed. "One moment."

He sprang shakily to the phone, made arrangements with his office, ducked into his room and came out again in no time flat, all dressed and lugging a bag into which he was still stuffing fishing clothes. Five minutes later we were on our way, three hale and hearty fellows.

Aptly named the "white fox," the bonefish has a number of unusual physical features which make it a strong contender for the place of the world's best game fish. The most conspicuous of these features is what scientists describe as an "inferior mouth"—that is, the upper mandible overlaps the lower so that the fish can root into the bottom of the ocean for its food. It is this rooting process which tips the fish up at such an angle that the tail protrudes above the water, waving back and forth with the movement of the fish, to perform the action termed "tailing" by bonefish anglers.

The young of this strange species pass through the same singular metamorphosis as the conger eel and the ladyfish. For a time they are elongate, ribbonlike, and transparent, with a small head and loose tissues. From this stage, they become gradually shorter and more compact, shrinking from 3 or 3½ inches to 2 inches in length and taking the form of the adult bonefish. The adult is a very beautiful fish, streamlined in every feature of his striking, silvery body. The hard-plated head with its overslung jaw

94

and eyes protected by a plasticlike lens adds still more to the appearance of speed.

Bonefish do not reach a great weight at any time. A 13-pound, 12-ounce fish taken by B. F. Peek, while fishing off Bimini, held up as the world-record bonefish from 1919 until 1948. Then Gert. Johannes Schmidt, fishing off Durban, South Africa, on April 8, 1948, landed a bonefish that weighed 15 pounds, 14 ounces, This new world-record bonefish had a length of 36 inches and a girth of 18¼ inches. On the thirtieth of November of the same year, Charles M. Cooke III came up with a bone that weighed an even 16 pounds. Cooke took his big fish off West Molokai, Hawaii. It had a length of 38 inches and a girth of 17⅛ inches. According to the International Game Fish Association, Cooke's fish stands as the present All Tackle bonefish record.

Fish which top these weights have, of course, been taken in nets—fish weighing 18, 20, and 22 pounds. But so far, these gigantic members of the species have escaped the nets and gaffs of the sport fisherman, and when a 20-pounder is taken on a fly, the angler who does it will have an experience that will probably leave him with a permanent look of astonishment on his face. Because if they fight in proportion to their smaller brothers, it will be almost impossible to land one. On the Florida Keys, where the bonefish is best known to light-tackle anglers, the average weight taken on a fly rod is from 6 to 7¼ pounds.

My own first bonefish was taken near Islamorada on the Keys, and weighed 8 pounds. For some time after that, I kept count of my take and out of some 250 fish landed, I estimated that only four were over 10 pounds. Of the same number, incidentally, I retained only five, one weighing 9 pounds, 2 ounces, which won the bonefish fly-rod class in the Metropolitan Miami Fishing Tournament in 1948; another weighing 10 pounds, 1½ ounces, which established a new tournament record the following year for bonefish taken on a fly; a third, taken off Islamorada in the fall of 1948, weighing 10 pounds, 9 ounces; then, in a single day, in November, 1949, two bones that were extra large fish—10 pounds, 7½ ounces and 11 pounds, 5½ ounces, the latter being, at that time, the unofficial world record for bonefish taken on a fly.

Those last two fish were taken on a day when big bonefish were everywhere. Captain Jimmie Albright had found where a school of bigger-than-usual fish were, and with his wife Frankee and my wife Mary and myself, went in search of them. In that one day, Jimmie and I took four bones over 10 pounds, although strangely enough, before that there were, as far as could be known, only two bones weighing over 10 pounds ever caught on flies. These were the 10-pound, 1½-ounce and the 10-pound, 9-ounce fish that I had caught. And to show that better-than-average fish really were cruising in that school, Jimmie guided Belle and Al Mathers to them, and Belle took one that weighed 10 pounds, 2 ounces and Al came through with a fine fish of 10 pounds, 12½ ounces.

That 11-pound, 5½-ounce fish of mine looked big. However, since then my fish has been beaten. On March 4, 1949, Herb Welsh, famous Maine fly caster, accompanied by Julian Crandall, president of the Ashaway Line and Twine Manufacturing Company, went out with Captain Albright and landed a bone that weighed 12 pounds, 4 ounces. So the fly-fishing bonefish story goes on and up, and I predict that it will not be long before the United States coastal record of 12 pounds, 14½ ounces will be beaten by a wielder of a fly rod.

For record purposes, four other fish of 10 pounds or better have been landed on flies. James F. Thornburg of South Bend, Indiana, fished with Captain Rolie Hollenbeck at Tavernier and landed a 10-pound, 5-ouncer; and Captain Bill Smith guided W. P. Langworthy of Philadelphia, Pa., to a 10-pound, 7-ounce fish, and Luis de Hoyos, Jr., of Monticello, N. Y. to a bonefish that went 10 pounds even. Then in the summer of 1950, Frankee Albright, famous woman guide of Islamorada, fly rodded into submission a 10-pound, 13½-ounce bonefish.

I didn't attempt to keep a record of the fish that got away or of those that hit and were on for only a short time, or that I lost after longer periods. But I think that it is safe to say that I lost almost as many as I landed. There are so many ways to lose a bonefish, most of them but quick. Such underwater impedimenta as sea fans, sea urchins, and other aquatic growths can cut through the leader in a second.

Along the Atlantic Coast, bonefish reach as far north as Cape Cod, Massachusetts, but they are most common off the Florida Keys. They also occur in the Bahamas, Bermuda, Haiti, Cuba, the Dominican Republic, and in most of the southern seas, and on the West Coast in California as far north as Monterey Bay. Their greatest concentration in the Pacific is in the Hawaiian Islands, and as previously mentioned, they are also found in South Africa. But for the purposes of this book, the flats or banks from Miami and Miami Beach south through the Florida Keys, where for certain geographic reasons bonefish reach their peak as a fly-rod fish, will serve as the basis for discussion.

In this area there exist certain conditions that are peculiarly suitable to the feeding of bonefish, since there are large expanses of water, which range from 6 inches to 3 feet in depth, according to the position of the tide. In this water the bottom is covered with crustaceans and there is also a good supply of killifish minnows upon which cruising bonefish feed. In addition to these ideal conditions, the banks are, in most places, readily accessible to the open sea and this, too, appears to me to be a factor in making the area popular with that very nervous and excitable gentleman, the admirable Mr. Bone.

Many anglers have fished this area for bonefish for years, with bait, but according to Captain J. T. Harrod of Miami, who was one of the first bonefish guides, no one apparently considered the bonefish as a fly-rod possibility. Captain Harrod reports, however, that in 1926 he guided Colonel L. S. Thompson of Red Bank, N. J. They fished at Long Key, using shrimp for bait, and had sport that Harrod still raves about. But when the tide wasn't right, they would hie themselves to nearby holes along the bonefish flats and fly-fish for baby tarpon. Colonel Thompson used Royal Coachman flies and caught tarpon right and left. But imagine their surprise when, while working on the small silver kings, they hooked and landed several bonefish.

"We thought it was accidental," J. T. said, "but we did catch quite a few that way. But think of going out onto the flats and fly cast for tailers? Not us. We just didn't think it could be done. Now it makes me wonder why we didn't realize that if they would hit a fly under such circumstances, well, it was a sure pop they would hit them when they were on the flats feeding."

One of the most thrilling sights in the world is to see a whole school of bonefish feeding in shallow water. They usually feed into the tide, nosing down into the grass in search of crabs and shrimp, with their tails waving above the water. Such tailers usually work in water not more than 18 inches deep—and the shallower the water, the more exciting the strike.

I was lucky enough to sit in on George M. L. La-Branche's first encounter with a bonefish via the fly-casting method, in just such thin water. LaBranche, internationally known angler and authority on trout and Atlantic salmon, had taken many bonefish on bait, but up to this time had not presented a fly to them. We went out, with Frankee Albright guiding, to fish the banks on the Gulf side of Islamorada. The water was glassy and when Frankee poled us out on the flat, the tide was so low that there was only 6 inches of water. I knew it was going to be a very tough job to even get close to a bonefish, much less hook one.

As Frankee poled us along, I watched LaBranche tie a white bucktail onto his 6-pound test leader. Then the canny angling veteran took up his line dressing and applied a liberal touch of it to the underside of the bucktail. He was taking no chances of that fly catching on the bottom in that shallow water.

Frankee spotted a bonefish tailing about a hundred feet

away and poled cautiously toward it. Its caudal fin flashed in the sunlight and once we saw the whole back as it slid over a thick growth of grass. At 60 feet LaBranche got ready to cast. At 50 he made a couple of false casts, then shot the fly out like a bullet and stopped his rod, dropping the fly lightly 2 feet in front of the tailing fish. It spied the fly at once and literally plowed up the sand to get to it. With a quick side thrust of his rod, LaBranche set the hook, and then we saw that grandest of all fishing sights, a bonefish in full flight across a flat of 6-inch water. He ran a good 400 feet and then brought out the full bag of bone-fish tricks while we watched his every move in that thin water. At last he was fought to a standstill, then gradually brought to boat. I heard Frankee say, as she slipped the net under him, "Congratulations, Mr. LaBranche. He'll go about 9 pounds." A 9-pound fish in 6 inches of water!

In water that is too deep for tailing, however, bonefish can be discovered almost as readily by the "muds" put up as the fish feed. Knowing about muds has saved the day for many an angler. I learned about them from Captain Jimmie Albright as he guided me across the flats one day. We had scoured the surface with no luck. Not a bonefish showed and the water looked dead. Aside from a couple of small sharks and a large sting ray drifting by, there had been no sign of underwater life.

"Let's get out of here," said Jimmie. "They're not on the flats. Let's head for deeper water and look for muds."

"What do you mean by 'muds'?" I asked.

He explained that as the bonefish root along the soft bottom in search of crabs and shrimp, they stir up little puffs of mud that rise to the surface and can be seen from

100

quite a distance. The mud that is distinctive of the bone-fish comes up in small round puffs which float away quickly in the direction the tide is moving. This is a feature to be remembered, as other fish also put up muds—particularly the sting ray, which, however, creates a large, deep-lying mud.

During a recent visit to Bermuda, I was talking about mudding bonefish to Louis Mowbray, curator of the Bermuda Aquarium, and I told him that I had watched them dig with their noses in the mud. "But that is not the only way they mud," he said.

"How else?" I wanted to know.

He led me into the aquarium and stopped before a tank in which a 2-pound bone was on display. The fish lay with his nose a couple of inches from the bottom, his body slanting upward at a 45-degree angle. As I watched, I saw a puff of sand arise in front of him.

"That's the way," Louis said. "They take water in their mouths and blow it out again. That way they disturb the mud and sand and find food."

As the fish feed, it is easy to plot their course by the muds, and it is often possible to take fish by casting just ahead of them. In doing so it is well to remember that the fish feed fast and therefore when you cast in front of them, be sure to lay the fly several yards beyond the last mud you see.

On the same day I mentioned above, I took my first mudding fish. I had my eye on a big round mud just ahead of us, which, however, had been made by a sting ray, when Jimmie shouted "Get ready! Quick! See those puffs coming up over there to the right!"

I spotted them at once.

"Cast a couple of yards in front of them," Jimmie said.

I did so and started the retrieve. Suddenly I saw a dark shape rush for the fly. I held my breath and waited for the strike. He hit and sprinted off toward the flat, then reversed and raced back past us. He was really stretching out and the line zizzed through the water a mile a minute.

I landed that baby, my first mudder, and since then I've taken many a mudding fish and it always gives me a thrill.

Bonefish are curious, too, and have a trick of following you the same way you follow them—by the trail of mud you put up as you wade. Sometimes they will come right up behind you, then see you and flush with a splash that scares the wits out of you. That happened one time when I was wading alone. I heard the splash and turned in time to see the fish speeding off. Then he stopped and swam back until he was within 30 feet of me, and started circling. Because of his peculiar actions, I was sure he was a shark. Once his dorsal fin showed as he went over a piece of up-jutting coral, and he looked like a 10-pounder. I kicked water in his direction and started to wade on. He followed, keeping his distance, but was definitely interested in me. I kicked water again and then as he flushed I saw him plainly. He was a big bonefish! How I cussed myself for my carelessness! The chances were against his hitting a fly, but who knows? The way that fish acted, he might have done anything. After that I made sure what fish it was I saw before I did any kicking.

If bonefish are neither tailing nor mudding, another way to spot them is to see the fish as they swim along under the water. This may sound easy to say and hard to do, but

102

it is possible to develop the faculty of seeing "through the water"—a practice that enables you to spot not only the bonefish you are seeking, but also many other interesting denizens of the shallow water, as you fish. The theory is that you look through the water, focusing on the bottom. In other words, don't allow your sight to stop at the surface, but let it go through, as if you were looking through glass, at the bottom. You will soon get onto it and you will be surprised how quickly you will begin to see fish which ordinarily would have escaped your eyes.

When you are fortunate enough to have the sun at your back, this system works much better. Trying to see swimming or even tailing fish, with the sun glaring in your eyes, is tough indeed. And for all this type of fishing, Polaroid glasses are indispensable, giving far greater vision into the water as well as protecting the eyes from glare.

Bonefish sometimes move in schools of fifteen or twenty. Again, they may swim in bunches of seven or eight. Or they may come cruising along in fours and fives. On occasion I have seen them pouring down the flats, literally by the hundred. Now and again you spot a single and these solitary swimmers are generally big fellows. The larger bonefish seem to go it alone, like rogue elephants. But however they are moving, the majority of strikes came at anywhere from 25 to 40 feet. Sometimes when you see a tailer well out, and are afraid of downing him by moving any closer, you can make a long cast to reach him. The same applies when fish are moving away from you. But on the whole, you will have far better results by casting to fish that are closer in.

At times they are slow and deliberate hitters and will

follow your fly in without taking a crack at it. Then, when they see you, they generally start slowly seaward, increasing speed as they go. In such cases, a cast in front of them will occasionally get a strike but on the whole, once the bonefish has seen you or suspects something unusual, he is gone. It is this extreme scariness in the bonefish which makes it essential that every cast should count. "One single cast to a fish" has become my slogan and it pays off heavily. This means that the approach of the fish must be judged very carefully and the cast made at just the proper time. No false casts to frighten the quarry, no futile casts made too soon, to catch on floating vegetation or on the bottom. Above all, no hasty casts that fall far short and must be speedily retrieved and recast before the fish gets too close. The fly must be in front of him while the fish is still far enough away to allow for a considerable follow before the strike. All too many times I've seen a fish flush at a line in the air, or follow the fly in too close and flush at the sight of a waving rod. The angler must be as steady as the bonefish is skittish!

And yet, there is always the exception! On a few occasions I have seen this usually nervous fish act as if he hadn't a fear in his whole body. I remember one time when I was wading on the ocean side of Key Largo. The tide was extremely low and I was at least 100 feet out from the mangrove-bordered shore line, yet wading in water that was scarcely 4 inches deep. Far in at the mangroves I saw a tail flip up. A fish was working the shore line in the same direction I was going, and a bit in front of me. I hurried in, on an angle, so as to be ahead of him when I came within casting range.

I was so sure that he would flush in that shallow water that I started my casts from 60 feet away. But although my first two offerings fell only 3 feet in front of him, he ignored them and continued on his way, stopping every few seconds to probe the bottom. I had to wade right along to keep up with him. He scoffed at the next three casts, too, but began to move a bit faster. Now I almost had to run to equal his pace and the splashing which marked my progress rang in my ears and must have been quite audible to him. Yet he remained undisturbed. Finally, after I had made about fifteen casts, some of them pretty sloppy, too, he socked that fly and tore out seaward, tossing water high in the air. In very short order he ran the line around a piece of coral and cut the leader.

That fish certainly heard me long before he hit. Most members of the species would not have looked at a fly after such a commotion.

Jimmie Albright and his wife Frankee probably had the honor of meeting the most exceptional bonefish of all! Jimmie had cast to the fish and the two of them watched it follow the retrieve. It came up slowly, sank down in the water a bit, and then took the fly on the top of its nose. Jimmie kept on retrieving. Then the fish dropped back and the fly slid off his nose, and as Jimmie kept it moving, followed it, first going to one side and then to the other. Then once more he took it on his nose. Finally, when the fly was within 10 feet of the boat, the bonefish saw Jimmie and swam slowly away. What that particular fish had in his mind is anyone's guess. Certainly he wasn't hungry and my opinion is that he was attracted by the white bucktail going past him and just wanted to play a bit. Jimmie has seen thousands of bonefish follow and hit lures but that was the first such performance he had ever been in on.

In order to understand the strike of a bonefish to a fly, a bit of explanation of their dental equipment might help. On the tongue, which is set well back in the mouth, the bonefish has teeth that have the appearance of small pebbles. On the roof of the mouth are three bands of hard muscle, running from the rear toward the front. They are about 2 inches long, and very hard. When the bonefish grabs a crab or other crustacean, he crushes it between these upper dental works and the hard, pebbly tongue before swallowing it. When picking a bonefish up with a finger inserted in his gill, you can sometimes feel the power of these crushers.

Knowing how he kills his prey allows you to time the strike better. When he hits, he usually hesitates a moment before throwing the fly back into the crushers and if you should strike at the moment he hesitates, you would pull the lure right out of his mouth. This is especially true when he is following the fly and pointing right at you. So, in the majority of cases, hold the strike until you feel him.

However, when a bonefish is coming fast for your fly, you don't have to wait. Usually he hits it so hard that he hooks himself. It's the slower taker you have to wait for. Again, sometimes you will see a bit of slack line straightening, before you feel the pull, and in such a case it is safe to strike. But usually it pays to wait even when you can actually see the fish take the fly.

Tailing fish, being definitely on the feed, respond much more readily than swimmers. The fly should be dropped

106

within a couple of feet and immediately in front of the tailers as they move from one grassy spot to another, along the sandy bottom. Feeding as they do, with their heads down, it is amazing how often they will see the lure. On occasion when they are grubbing so hard that they do not see it, the fly may be retrieved in the usual manner, without commotion, and a cast back to the same fish will generally be spotted.

When fishing a school of tailers, it is often possible to pick out the largest fish by the size of the tail and make a cast directly to him. Sometimes the smaller ones in the school will beat him to the lure, but more often a well-placed cast will take the big one. But when bonefish are in schools and you present a fly to them, they often flush because of the fact that several of them will make a lunge for the fly at the same time, bump into each other, and especially in really shallow water, become scared and take out of there in a hurry.

Once I was out with Red Greb on an afternoon when schools of bonefish were everywhere. We'd cast to them; they would bump into each other and flush. In shallow water, when a school of bonefish flush they take off in a series of explosions that is nerve shattering to say the least. First one will flush with a loud pop and a boil of water. Then fish will start plopping all around and you can follow their course as they push water in front of them, heading for the deep. Then, when your nerves are settled and you begin looking for more fish—then, and there is always one—a bonefish with a strange sense of humor will burst out right at your feet and just about finish you off completely. On the afternoon I am describing, after three such performances, Red turned to me.

"There are too many bonefish here," he mumbled. "Let's go somewhere else."

Never had I thought to hear such words from a bone-fisherman!

In fishing for tailers, another point to remember is that the bonefish is particularly nervous when he is crossing sandy patches on the bottom. They must know that they are conspicuous when they pass over these places and they sweep across as if headed for some distant sea. If there is a ripple on the water, this scariness is not so pronounced but nevertheless it is better at all times to wait for the fish to come within casting range. In this way you avoid the chance of flushing them by any inadvertent noise or splashing of the water. In addition, since bone-fish rarely swim any great distance with the caudal fin out of water, this waiting policy gives you the opportunity of charting their course as they tail, then swim a while, and then tip up again when they discover more food.

Bonefish feed on minnows as well as crustaceans and such fish, cruising along in search of their prey, generally swim faster than tailers and as a rule do not show so much interest in lures. Sometimes they will follow the fly for 20 or 30 feet, trying to decide whether or not they want it. It pays, at such times, to give the fly a quick, 6-inch jerk. The bonefish apparently thinks the minnow, or whatever he imagines it to be, is trying to escape, and will be teased into striking. I've had many a bonefish follow a steady retrieve right to my feet and then refuse it, but that 6-inch jerk really gets them. They hit it hard, seeming

108

The author with the world-record (fly-rod) striped bass taken at Coos Bay, Oregon. The big striper socked a white popping bug and battled forty minutes before being boated. *Photo by* Coos Bay (Oregon) Times.

Fishing the surf at Bermuda for the scrappy and dashing gaff-topsail pompano. Along any of Bermuda's beautiful pink beaches fine sport can be had with the surf-racing pompano by merely wading in and casting. The clearness of the water allows you to spot your fish and make your cast directly to him. *Bermuda News Bureau, Photo by Higgs.*

to spring on it, and every fish taken in that manner seems to be well hooked.

While as a general rule bonefish like a slow retrieve—just fast enough to keep the hook from fouling on the bottom—there are notable exceptions to the rule. Sometimes schools of bonefish are seen sweeping across the flats. Thy make such a commotion in the water that they can be spotted from a distance. Perhaps they have finished feeding and are heading for a resting place or perhaps a fast-dropping tide is making them scurry to safety. Certainly they are traveling at a much faster pace than usual. Under such conditions, a quick toss ahead of them and a very fast retrieve will frequently take a fish. On the other hand, I have also seen bonefish from such a school follow, take a fly, and then eject it again. A fish in one school to which I cast did this three times, finally leaving the fly altogether, while I stood there open mouthed and desperate. The same thing happened again later, so I struck the next one the minute he took. The fly, as I had expected, pulled right out of his mouth and I let it stay still for a moment before starting the retrieve. He repeated and took it in his mouth, only to eject it once more. I kept the fly coming and suddenly, from only 15 feet away, he socked it so hard he almost knocked the rod out of my hand!

But fish from these fast-traveling schools usually hit savagely, detaching themselves from the school and socking the fly while still moving at the speed of the other fish. The fish sees something good to eat and wants to get it in a hurry and rejoin his onrushing mates. The fast retrieve is absolutely necessary if you want to catch fish from these schools. They are scurrying along at a rapid pace and if you cast your fly and allow it to just float in the water, or do not retrieve it at a speed faster than the fish are moving, they will think it is just a bit of grass or other matter floating in the water. They need to see it moving faster than they are, to realize that it is something good to eat.

When a bonefish is hooked, he usually starts for deep water. He doesn't leap or jump as so many fish do, but travels at express-train speed, usually in a straight line. His first run may be 200 or 300 feet. It may be 400. Some of the bigger ones even run 500 or 600. And while that run is in progress, it is never safe to touch the reel. Set the drag before you begin to fish and when the bone hits and starts out, raise the rod as high as you can, straight up over your head. Never allow it to drop and point toward the fish or he may make a sudden lunge and break the leader. When the rod is held straight up, its natural pliancy will work to your advantage. The height will also help to keep your line and leader from catching on sea fans and underwater growths.

If the fish runs around a sea fan and stops, do not pull back on the rod. The extra pressure might be all that is needed to cut the leader or allow him to pull loose. Move toward the fish, keeping a steady pressure on, until you are in a position to free the line. If you cannot do this, try to figure out from which side the fish took the line around the obstacle. Work away from that side and frequently the line will fall free and the fish will start to swim away. Still another method is to give slack and hope that the fish will take off again, freeing the line as he does so.

Once, while wading at Key Largo, I hooked a bonefish

110

that tore off seaward a mile a minute, then started going around things. I held my rod high and didn't pull back, just kept a tight line and started reeling in as I walked toward the fish. Finally I got to where the casting line was under a sea fan. I shoved my rod to the side and pulled. The line came loose and I reeled fast, taking up slack. Twenty feet away the line went to the bottom again and I started reeling once more and walking in that direction. Hearing a splash some distance off, I looked up and saw the fish just under the surface and 50 feet off to my left. I hoped he wouldn't have strength enough left to break the leader against the sea fan, around which it was wrapped. I got the line off that one and then saw that it was around another one only 5 feet away. It looked hopeless but I kept reeling, walking, releasing line, taking up slack, and finally everything was free and the fish was still on!

Such adventures don't always end so fortunately. Once I gave Charlie Ebbets a new GAF line. We had no sooner started fishing when Charlie saw a bone, tossed a fly to it, and had a hit. The fish was in shallow water and tore off to sea, throwing water about and whipping line off the reel like anything. Charlie's new fly line dashed through the rod guides and the backing tore out after it. Then, zingo! The line went slack, and shrugging his shoulders, Charlie started to reel in. In came the backing—then—nothing! That new fly line was bound for points east. The fish evidently cut it on a sharp piece of coral. But that's bonefishing. Things happen.

All of which reminds me of another occasion when a bonefish helped himself to a line. Monk Montague and I were wading the flats on Key Largo. Just before we went out Monk had asked me how to tie his new fly line to the backing.

"Give it to me," I said. "I'll tie it together with a barrel knot."

I did. The first fish Monk hooked went running down the shore line a mile a minute, while Monk held on. The casting line left the rod tip and just then it left the backing, too. That knot I had tied!

"Oh boy!" I thought. "A new line, too."

Then I saw Monk rushing ahead, throwing water all about. He stooped down and came up with the end of the fly line in his hands.

"He's still on!" he cried. "What will I do now?"

"Hand-line him in," I shouted.

Monk pulled back and the bonefish started in high at the same moment. The leader snapped as if it had been a strand of spider web.

"You can't hand-line those things!" Monk muttered as he waded ashore, sat down on a piece of coral, and tied his line and backing together with a barrel knot, and didn't even so much as ask my advice on how to do it.

Bonefish can take you over the hurdles in many different ways. With Harry Snow, famous bonefish guide, I fished a flat that was particularly heavy with mangroves. The very first tail Harry spotted was right in the middle of a dense growth. It was so thick that we had to follow the fish for 20 feet before I could cast. Finally we spied an opening and I dropped the fly in front of the fish and had a hit at once. He took off through the mangroves, while I held the rod up, trying to steer the line over 3-foot high trees.

112

Then, in his frenzied flight that fish ran smack through the inverted V-shaped root of a mangrove bush and there we were, the fish on one side and the rod and I on the other. Still he kept going, taking more line all the time, and only stopped after he had line and leader wrapped around several other roots. But strangely enough, that maneuver of his saved the day for me. While keeping a tight line, I managed to stick the tip of the rod through the V-shaped root, and hand over hand, pulled the entire rod through. I don't know why the fish didn't get off during all that business, but he didn't, and before long Harry netted him.

However, it is not too often that such difficulties are encountered, as many of the flats have smooth bottoms with patches of grass and a gradual slope, usually free of obstructions.

Bonefish feed best when the tide is running its swiftest, as apparently in the moving water they can scent their quarry much better than in still water. At dead low tide they are sometimes found in shallow water, either in schools or singly, hugging the sandy holes among the grassy patches. They are evidently resting and will remain motionless until you are right on top of them. However, you must be able to see them from quite a distance in order to catch them under these conditions.

There are two recognized ways of fishing for bonefish—by wading and by boat.

Wading calls for good eyes and the ability to move quietly in the water. The angler moves along slowly in knee-deep water, watching for muds or for tailing fish. He must also keep a sharp eye immediately in front of him as cruising fish will sometimes appear so quickly that there is no time for a cast before they flush. When the fish are spotted swimming toward you, it is important to get the lure out at once so there is room for a follow before they see you. Once a bonefish knows you are there, he will look at you with a cold and fishy eye and swim slowly away. Once they see you they seldom strike. Make a long cast and give them plenty of time to look it over.

While wading for bonefish, it is profitable to make regular, fairly long pauses. Standing still allows you to see fish which you might miss while moving. Bonefish often slip inshore from the angler and from a stationary position it is much easier to pick out moving objects. In such a case, the cast is often made into water only 8 or 10 inches deep and the fly should be dropped well in front of and beyond the fish, and the retrieve timed so that the fly crosses a few feet in front of the quarry. The bonefish is easily frightened in such shallow water and if the cast is laid in too close, the fish will flush wildly. The exception to this rule comes when the fish are tailing. Then, I drop the fly just 2 feet in front of them.

When a scared bonefish darts away in that thin water, it's a sight to behold! He goes out in a burst of speed that leaves you as startled as a man at a tea party when his suspenders break, staring popeyed at a trail of bubbles and flying sand. You just can't believe a fish can move so fast!

Fishing one of the flats on the ocean side of Key Largo, I had a fight with a bonefish that is as vivid as if it had happened yesterday. Sifford Pearre, of Baltimore, and his son Sifford, Junior, were fishing with me. Nelson Edwards was also along, taking movies. We had just finished lunch and I waded out with the intention of working down the shore into the tide. When I was hardly knee-deep, I saw the tip of a tail out of the corner of my eye. I cast several feet in front of where the fish was and had only made one foot-long strip when he struck. He hit near the surface and threw water high in the air as he ran straight out for a hundred feet, then started a looping slice to the right. My backing zipped from the reel and I expected the fish to start slowing down. He continued on. I felt fairly secure as I had 600 feet of backing. But the way that baby kept going and the way the line kept hopping off the reel core had me worried. I tightened a little but that didn't faze him a bit. He kept right on at that same terrific pace.

I had been holding my rod as high as I could to keep the line from catching on sea fans or sea urchins. I lowered it, hoping that the extra pressure from the line in the water would slow him down. It didn't. The tide was fairly low and I knew that flat. It was time, I decided, to take off after him if I wanted to land him at all. I started wading as fast as I could. Line still kept slipping from the reel. I splashed on, hoping that he would slow down before all my backing was gone.

Finally he did ease up a little. He still bored on but that wild dash was broken. I figured that he had made 600 feet on that run, in what seemed to be about six seconds.

I tried, then, to get him coming my way but he had other ideas. He headed back in the direction from which he had come and stayed away out and I just couldn't get him in. I waded after him, holding my own but not gaining

115

an inch. Glancing back to where Pearre and Nelson were, I was surprised to see how far down the shore the chase had taken me. I increased my pace and got back some line, and then had him swimming my way. I reeled fast and kept him coming. Then he turned and started again for deep water. He ran about a hundred feet this time, taking all the line I had been able to regain, before I stopped him. Once again he dogged it toward his starting point while I cranked and cranked. I managed to get some line back and for a while held him stationary in the water as I walked toward him, reeling as fast as possible. He started again and this time we stayed even. Our march was drawing us closer to our starting point. I could hear faint shouts from young Sifford. The end of my casting line appeared above the water and I breathed more easily. But suddenly he was off again, headed straight for shore this time. This was bad. The tide was lower and I was afraid of the sea fans and sea urchins and sponges that were there. He might cut the leader on them or run around one and pull loose. But I brought him around finally, and looking up, saw that we were back within 20 yards of where we had started.

He began to circle. Around and around he went and I wasn't able to get him in. Finally he weakened and I put on more pressure. He came fast now. He was almost finished. I raised my rod and pulled the fish toward me. He turned on his side and I reached down to pick him out of the water.

I don't know what made me look up, but I did, and what I saw almost gave me heart failure. A shark that was at least 9 feet long was coming fast, headed straight

116

for that bonefish. He was right there! I kicked hard in the water right at the shark's nose. I didn't hit him but the splash of water, and no doubt my sudden movement, turned him and he started back seaward at the same rapid pace. I watched him go, then slipped my hand under the bonefish and waded ashore with him. He weighed 9 pounds, 2 ounces and the fight he put up lasted for fifty minutes. That's a scrap that stands out.

When bonefish, either in schools, small groups, or singly, are seen swimming parallel to the shore line, the cast should be dropped on the seaward side. Their approach to a fly on that side seems readier than to one laid on the shore side, and they seem less scared and hit more boldly. They evidently know that safety lies in that direction and are less cautious when moving toward the deep water. Often when you take a fish from such a school, he will continue right along with the rest. If the school slows down, so does the hooked fish. If they swing right or left, so does he. Finally the school will sense something wrong, either from the antics of the hooked fish or from the line or leader brushing into them. Then they flush and head for the deep, the hooked fish along with them, and your fight begins.

Another method of catching bonefish while wading is to locate just off a small point. The ideal spot is one where there is a patch of sand with areas of grass on either side. Take a comfortable stance in knee-deep water and wait for the fish to come to you. Since bonefish feed into the tide and parallel to the shore line, then, whether cruising or tailing, they must make it around the point. Standing in one spot like that gives you all the advantages—the fish must come, you have a minimum of water disturbance, and your eyes have time to become accustomed to the surrounding bottom and thus enable you to locate the fish better.

I'll never forget the time I was wading around a point and inshore from me saw a bonefish swimming along. I tossed a fly to him and watched him swim by it without seeming to give it a glance. As I looked after him with disgruntled feelings, something almost yanked my rod from my hands. I kept looking where the fish had been and wondering how he had ever hit my fly when he had just gone past it. Line was slipping from my reel and the scream of the click finally brought me to my senses. I got into the fight and eventually landed a nice fish. While I fought him, it dawned on me that the strike had been from another fish which I had not seen—and which I probably would have seen if I had stopped for a while, off that point, and cased the water as I have just been describing.

While fishing in this same manner, most anglers also keep casting out toward the deeper water, at the same time watching the terrain in front of them as they strip the line. Sometimes this blind casting will take a fish which may have seen the angler and moved to deeper water, or may simply be cruising at that level. Such blind casting is not too much fun as it is slow and tiring, but it does pay off. And frequently, while stripping in your line after such a seaward cast, you will see a swimmer headed your way and will be able to pull your line out readily for a quick cast to the oncoming fish, in plenty of time for the strike.

How important it is to remain quiet was brought home

118

to me very forcibly on a wading trip on the flats at Key Largo. After wading about half a mile without seeing a fish, my wife Mary grew tired and said she was going to stand on a nearby point and wait for the fish to come to her. I went on. Just a short distance away, however, I heard her cry "I see a tailer! I see a tailer!" and I stopped to watch her cast to the fish. Then, out of the corner of my eye I saw a bonefish lying motionless in the water not 10 feet away from me! I tossed my fly to him and watched him follow it a foot, then swim slowly away. When he had put about 20 feet between us, I made a back-hand cast with my arm held down so as not to show motion, and the fish hit it at once. Before Mary stopped on the point, we hadn't seen a fish. But as soon as we both stood still, fish appeared.

Dick Splaine, the fever patient described in the opening lines of this chapter, hooked three fish in one day in one of the best bits of blind casting I have seen. Dick had perfected his Squeteager fly for large sea trout and did so well with it on them that he naturally wanted to try it on bonefish. I offered him the pick of my fly box, but knowing fly tiers as I do, I was not surprised that he turned them all down. He had his pet fly and he wanted to use it. There was one hitch to it, and I knew it, but I said nothing.

As the tide was low, we waded well out from shore before starting to cast. I left Dick on the point, tossing his fly seaward and working very hard indeed. It wasn't long before I heard a cry and looking back, saw Dick's rod bobbing down, and noticed the wake the bonefish was making in the shallow water. Then the fish hung up

119

and Dick started after him. The bonefish was struggling and throwing water about in an effort to get off, and Dick was trying his best to free it from whatever it was caught on. "Caught" it was, I knew, because Dick had tied that Squeteager with tandem hooks, and I knew that one of them was swinging free and had caught on some under-water growth. Dick landed that fish somehow or other, but not before it had got free from one obstruction only to immediately catch on another. I watched Dick wade ashore and do things to one of those hooks. After that he caught two more fish, and this time he didn't get hung up.

Skiff fishing, particularly if your boat is handled by an expert bonefish guide, gives considerably more mobility than wading. Oars are dispensed with, as any splashing or creaking of the oarlocks would frighten the quarry. The guide stands up and poles the boat across the flats until he spots a fish. Then he places the angler within range and crouches down. Otherwise, the same rules apply as in wading.

J. T. Harrod, mentioned earlier in this chapter, is a past master at handling a skiff, and on one trip to the flats off Cape Florida, he gave me an exhibition of fine and fancy polework that was a pleasure to be in on. The things he did with that skiff in a 15-mile breeze were wonderful. Bonefish seemed to appear in front of me from nowhere, always down wind, and all I had to do was make a short cast, set the hook, and fight the fish. On one such cast, the fish followed the fly for what seemed to me an unusually long time. I kept stripping the line in as slowly as possible, hoping that the fish would not see the boat and flush. I slowed my retrieve still more, barely moving

120

the fly in the water. The bone was right in back of the fly the whole time, giving it the eye and doing nothing about it. Then I gave a short, 6-inch jerk, and he piled all over it. I struck and the fight was on. Later, Allen Corson, who was along, said, "J. T., that was really a perfect performance. The way you kept poling the skiff away as that bone followed the fly was something to see."

No wonder the fish hadn't flushed! With his quiet poling, J. T. had lengthened my retrieve by some 20 feet and allowed the fish time to make up his mind to hit.

On the whole, I believe that skiff fishing pays off better as it is easier to pole quietly than to wade quietly within casting distance, and therefore your lure can be presented to more fish.

Tailing and swimming fish are also more readily spotted when the angler has the added height of the boat and the height aids, too, in keeping the line clear of underwater growth while the fish is being played. And if need be, you can follow the fish in any water, if he should threaten to exhaust the backing on your reel.

There are many, many things that may affect your success in bonefishing. Some flats produce more strikes on the incoming tide while others pay off when the tide is on its way out. Such circumstances are discovered only through fishing the particular area concerned, or from local fishermen and bonefish guides. The single consistency in bonefish behavior, in this regard, seems to be that they hit best on the outgoing tide from halfway out until slack, and on the incoming tide from when it starts in until the three-quarter mark. This seems to hold good on all flats.

It is tough to take fish from flats that have a lot of bird life. Cormorants, pelicans, the great white heron, and others flying over, wading, or floating on the flats will make bonefish very scary. So if there is a choice, it is always better to select a flat that does not have excessive bird life. However, it does pay to follow the course of a single, low-flying bird, as it will sometimes flush a covey of bonefish that you have not seen. You can then watch them as they run through the shallow water and finally they will settle and begin to feed again. After resting them long enough for them to get over their fright, a careful stalk will give you the opportunity to take fish from a school that you might otherwise have missed.

It is also a good idea to cast behind any rays that you see swimming over the flats. With them there are usually a few fish that follow along in hopes of snatching a stray morsel dug up by the ray. I have hooked a number of bonefish by just such casts into the ray's mud, or a foot or so behind him as he swims.

Windy days can add to the bonefisherman's troubles, too. I recall one time when I was casting downwind from the stern of a skiff while my guide held the boat against a stiff breeze. I spotted an enormous bonefish, cast to him, and he took. As he took I set the hook, and then looked down to see where my slack line was. It was around the motor in a perfect loop. Before I could get it loose, the bonefish snapped the leader and made off with the fly. The guide said he would have weighed more than 11 pounds.

Still another time, I cast to a school of bonefish charging by and saw one of them detach himself from the rest and take the lure. As he started seaward, I felt the line around my wrist. I struggled in vain to get it off. The line tightened, the rod tip bowed down, and zippo! off he went with the fly. The sad part of that one was that I didn't get another strike that afternoon and the following morning I was leaving for the north for the summer. I carried thoughts of that encounter with me and vowed that it wouldn't happen again. But from time to time it has, and I guess as long as there is wind, it always will. Everything must be right when you tangle with a bonefish.

Since very few people eat bonefish, and most of them are returned to the water unharmed, little need be said about conservation. Those who fish for them often become so fond of this sporty species that, as Howard Cox of Cincinnati said, "I'd just as soon eat a relative."

In closing I would like to stress again the extreme nervousness of this species. Bonefish are frequently frightened off a flat by too many rods fishing it too hard for too many days in a row. They will either stay out in deep water or go farther afield, and several days' rest is needed before they will return to that feeding ground. The angler, therefore, who plunges up and down the flats trying to cover as much ground as possible, is disregarding the principal requirements of bonefishing and is at the same time destroying the flat as a fishing ground for himself and for others.

Bonefish are fly-taking fish, all right, though at times diffident ones. But when they do make up their minds, they give their all in their dash to engulf the lure. Picking the right fly for bonefish is a question of picking the fly for the water level and for the time of year, rather than choosing one specific pattern for all times. During the winter months from December to the middle of March, they like a white bucktail tied on a 1/0 hook. They like streamers, too, during this period, but the streamers with white feathers, such as the Upperman #101 or #108 really come into their own during the period from the fifteenth of March through to the end of July.

The advantage of the white bucktail at any time when fishing flats that are shallow is that bucktail hairs, being hollow, float better than the streamers which, in such thin water, often sink and catch on the bottom.

During the months from August to the end of October, a very small fly, such as those tied by Jimmie Albright and Bill Smith, seems almost a necessity to bring strikes from bones. These flies are only an inch long and are tied on #1 hooks. The larger flies seem to frighten the bone-fish, making them flush not only when in the water, but even at the sight of the fly in the air. It was only after repeated refusals by bones to the larger flies that Jimmie and Bill tied the smaller ones. They worked, and then life was more bearable at Islamorada.

8.

Tarpon

THE SILVER KING

F<small>LY FISHING</small> for tarpon is plenty sporty but the yield in landed fish is poor. Veteran fly-fishermen say that on fish up to 15 pounds, the average is two fish landed for every ten hooked. On fish from 15 to 20 pounds, they expect to land two out of twenty hooked. From 25 pounds up, one fish out of forty is above the average. Such figures give an idea of what to expect when you tangle with this great fighting machine.

The tarpon packs tremendous power in his body and the inside of his mouth is as hard as concrete. Setting a hook in that mouth is something like trying to stop the charge of a water buffalo with a pea shooter. He also has a rough edge to his mouth and has extremely sharp scales and gill covers, any one of which may saw through the leader. Usually, after you hook a tarpon it is just a matter of seconds before the hook is thrown or one of these hazards has won out against you. But while you have him on, he is unleashed dynamite—a leaping, flashing, somer-saulting silver powerhouse. And quite aside from the physical features of the fish, you lose plenty of baby tarpon because of their trick of jumping over the ever present

125

mangrove branches, boring into the mangrove roots, and snapping the leader on them. When a tarpon, whatever his size, really decides to go somewhere, there isn't a lot you can do about it. You can hope, and that is about all.

While little is authoritatively known regarding the spawning habits of the tarpon, it is believed that they go into fresh water for this purpose. Some ichthyologists hold that the young go through a transparent larval stage similar to the metamorphosis of the bonefish. However, as far as I am aware, this theory has not been substantiated. I do know, though, that 6- and 7-inch tarpon have been caught in fresh-water parts of the Everglades, and I have seen one of these small tarpon about 6 inches long and weighing 2 ounces. It had been caught on a specially contrived fly at Marco, by Fausto Nieva of Miami, in 1949. Since then I believe Dave Newell, famous outdoorsman, landed one weighing 1½ ounces—also in the Everglades. At any rate, there is an abundance of tiny tarpon in Florida waters, seeming to indicate that they do spawn there.

The smaller fish appear to stay in one locality until they reach a weight of 10 or 15 pounds. At that time they begin short migrations, moving along the coast and throughout the Gulf of Florida.

No one can say just how big a tarpon is when he joins the hordes which, during the months of May, June, and July, migrate to the West Coast of Florida and then go on to Texas and the other Gulf states. Because of the fact that so many of the fish remain in Florida waters, it is hard to put a finger on the size or age of the tarpon when they first go on this western visit. In any event, there are always enough of them left to make good fly-fishing, all year round.

While this westward trek provides equally exciting deep-water tarpon fishing for many other parts of the southern United States, the species does not frequent shallow waters in those areas, and therefore does not lend itself so readily to fly-fishing. But in Florida there is good fly-fishing for tarpon almost everywhere—in ditches and canals, in the Gulf of Mexico and the Gulf of Florida, and along both coasts. They travel in schools and in small groups. They are in the shallow places in the Gulf, in the channels and little holes bordering the bonefish flats. They lie in the shade under the mangrove trees. At times they are in the inlets under the bridges along the Overseas Highway on the Keys. They go up the rivers and work through the canals all over southern Florida. In parts of the Gulf of Florida, where they stay all year, they have been termed "yardfish" or "dockfish," so consistently do they haunt certain spots. One time I went out with the well-known tarpon and bonefish guide, Captain Jimmie Albright, at Islamorada. As we left the dock, he said, "What size tarpon do you want to fish for?"

"What do you mean?" I asked.

"Well," he said, " I know some spots where you can cast to 10-pounders. Farther on I know where there are 25- and 50-pounders. Another place I know of, there are 100- and 150-pound fish."

Just like that! Name your own poison.

Mysterious as is their beginning, there is no guess as to the willingness of a tarpon to take a fly, nor as to his ability as a fighter. He is a great fish on any tackle and reaches his peak when hooked on fly-fishing gear. Fly fishing for tarpon is rough and rugged and exciting. No other fish gives you quite the same thrill or puts up a better battle.

The strike of a tarpon to a fly is one of the fastest of all piscatorial rises. He comes up in a looping roll, which shows you only a brief flash of his silvery sides as he hits the lure and starts down with it. He sucks the fly in as he comes up, and closes his mouth on it as he dives. If you strike while his mouth is open to suck the fly in, you will take it away from him. A possible exception to this is in the case of baby tarpon, where the strike is so fast that the wait is hardly appreciable. The name "baby tarpon," incidentally, was probably first applied by anglers who worked the canals and caught fish weighing anywhere from 2 to 10 pounds, but has gradually come into general usage to describe any tarpon up to 20 pounds. But don't be misled. There isn't anything babyish about a 20-pound, or even a much smaller, tarpon.

The building of roads in southern Florida resulted in a network of ditches paralleling the roads, created when the coral and dirt were dredged up to fill the road bed. Water moved into the ditches thus formed and into these canals came fish from nearby bays, and in some cases from the ocean. In fact, you never know what is going to hit your lure when you make a cast. Once, while fishing in a Key Largo canal for baby tarpon, I saw a dark shape under the popping bug I was using, following it along slowly. As I stared, the shadow rose up eerily and then a pair of bulging eyes broke the surface and looked at me. A moment later a 5-foot crocodile slashed at the

128

lure with his terrifying mouthful of teeth. I struck and the saurian dove, and I had him on for maybe a minute as he headed for the shelter of the mangrove roots. Then the line went slack and the popper rose to the surface. He must have been hooked in the teeth, because the leader wasn't damaged a bit. Or else he just opened that huge maw and let the bug float out. He came up again and lay under the mangroves with his snout sticking out, but repeated casts to him brought only disdain. Then he made a move in our direction and I felt something pulling at my sleeve and heard my wife's voice.

"I think" she said, "that there is a whole big school of baby tarpon rolling at the other end of the canal."

Along the Tamiami Trail, where the canal runs through the Everglades, on a week-end afternoon you may see as many as a hundred fly fishermen. It is an entertaining sight to stand in the road and watch the backcasts shooting out over it as cars from every state in the union whiz by. The angler is generally hidden from sight in an opening in the bushes along the water's edge and it is entirely up to him to be sure that the road is clear before he makes his backcast. On one occasion I was with Red Greb, the well-known Miami angler I have mentioned previously in these pages, on an occasion when he didn't look sharply enough. He had seen a car and waited, as he thought, long enough for it to pass and then had begun his backcast. What he failed to note was a small trailer hooked on the back of the car. His line wrapped around it and Red's reel began to screech. In great confusion, he tightened up and half of his line departed with the trailer. Many

129

another line has gone down that road, too, headed for Ohio or Illinois or other points west!

Fly-fishing the canals calls for a special technique. You cruise slowly along the road, watching the canal for signs of activity. When you see the bubbles or the big, ever widening circles that mark the roll of a school of tarpon, you park your car, put your gear together, and start fishing. Many a time I have seen car after car crawling along the Tamiami Trail, with anglers poking their heads out as they search the waters, and with rods sticking out at all angles, ready to spring into instant action.

If you are new to the particular canal that you are fishing, you can spot the best places by noting the openings in the trees or bushes which line the banks. Fishermen have forced these openings here and there so they will have room to cast and they are usually in the places most used by tarpon. Many of the canals also have open spaces where you can cast freely.

In canal fishing, casting must be very accurate, especially during the heat of the day when the tarpon are back under the mangroves. The fly should hit as close to them as possible, as an overshoot will mean that you are hung in the mangroves on the other side and will lose the fly. Yet if the cast is too short, you will not catch fish. The retrieve can also make or break the day's sport. In tarpon fishing, nothing ever happens to a smooth, even retrieve. You must impart plenty of action to the fly. After it has landed on the water, allow it to sink a bit, then manipulate the rod tip so that the fly comes back toward you in 6-inch jerks, increasing in speed as the fly nears the shore from which you are fishing. Play it right out to the bank, as

130

tarpon often follow a lure across the canal and hit it just as it is about to be lifted from the water. I have had many a strike right at my feet and have learned to be on the alert until the fly is in the air.

When tarpon are not rolling, you fish more or less blind. It's slower going, but still offers plenty of good sport. Drop the fly on the far side, let it sink a bit, then retrieve with the tip imparting those same short jerks to the fly. Throw back to the same spot repeatedly and more often than not you will coax out a fish from some unsuspected resting place. Take your time.

When a baby tarpon hits in these canal waters, he usually takes to the air at once. His jumps are apt to go in any direction but almost without fail he will end up tangled in the branches or roots of the mangroves. This is tough on leaders and even tougher on your supply of flies. But there is nothing you can do about it except put on all the pressure you dare, as soon as he hits, and try to keep him away from those obstacles. In the majority of cases you will be spared the worry anyway, because the tarpon sucks in your fly, jumps, and throws it! The leaps are so flashy and the fight so satisfactory that you won't care whether or not you land the fish. Tarpon fishing is strictly for fun, anyway, as they are not good food fish. A dead tarpon is just another dead fish. A live, leaping, scrapping one is insurance of future sport, and most anglers carefully remove the hook and return the fish to the water unharmed.

The 9½-foot rod more than proves its value in canal fishing, too. When a hooked tarpon dives under the mangroves, the 9½-footer will frequently allow you to get out far enough to clear the fish. Similarly, you can play him out in deeper water by thrusting the rod out in that direction, and then steer him through the brush and grasses sticking up near the shore. Many baby tarpon are lost in landing them and mostly because the light rods being used are not long enough to keep the fish out in the middle and away from mangrove roots. Another reason for the long rod is that in lots of ways it would be a shame to abuse a lighter stick in the rough casting from small openings in the trees along the banks, over low mangrove bushes, and in various other spots where, whether you watch it or not, your rod is going to slam into the bushes.

The best time to use poppers for tarpon in the canals is at, and for a short time after, daybreak, just before dark and during the night—if you care to fish at that time. Either due to the confined water area or because the noise of the popper frightens them, they just don't react to a popper in the daytime as well as they do in the open waters of bays and sounds. And maybe it is because of less aeration in the warmer waters of the canals, but whatever the cause, it doesn't pay to use a popper during the bright hours of the day. During the daytime the cork-bodied wounded minnows do much better. They represent the struggles of a live, wounded minnow trying to make his way along. That type of lure doesn't make the noise or the water disturbance that poppers do, and while they are not a cure-all for bringing strikes during the day, they will take fish for you. But with them, too, the best times to fish are the natural feeding times of early morning and late afternoon. The best lure to use during full day is a deep-riding streamer tied on a 3/0 hook.

On the gulf side of the Florida Keys, tarpon are found in so-called "lakes"—water from 8 to 12 feet deep, surrounded for the most part by the shallow banks upon which bonefish feed. Tarpon also hang out in the channels throughout the gulf and stay under the mangrove bushes bordering the numerous Keys. At dusk they leave the shade of the mangroves and the depths of the channels and cruise the thinner water in search of food.

This is a thrilling time to fish for them and on one trip to the channels at Tarpon Basin on Key Largo, Ray Shuey and I were treated to some of the greatest jumping I ever saw. They were small tarpon, but really on the active side. I was caught, on that trip, without any salt-water bugs, and was forced to use ordinary black-bass bugs. What those hard-mouthed tarpon did to the hooks was a caution. And we didn't land a single fish out of at least twenty-five hooked. They would hit, take to the air, and throw the hook. Seldom did we have any on after the first jump. When I stopped to look at the hook in my bug, I discovered that it was bent straight out. After that I looked at hooks that had been pushed into many weird shapes, but the fish were so much fun, hitting those bugs and leaping all over the place, that we didn't bother to change to streamers. But after that, my fishing bag always contained a couple of bugs with hooks capable of withstanding the crushing power of the tarpon.

In the lakes you usually see and cast directly to a chosen fish. Sometimes they are found cruising right under the surface, and at other times they go deeper. Occasionally you get strikes from fish you don't see, but generally, because of the clearness of the water, you can spy them.

Be sure to put the lure in front of the fish, as a cast that hits anywhere behind a tarpon will flush him.

In such lakes there will be tarpon weighing 25 and 50 pounds as well as some even reaching 150 pounds—and every one of them is ready to sock that lure. In fact, with the possible exception of Arctic grayling, tarpon are the fly-takin'est fish I've ever encountered. I remember one trip in particular, in April, 1949, when Harry Friedman, Charlie Ebbets, and I took Louis Mowbray, curator of the Bermuda Aquarium and Museum, out for a week end of fishing in the Gulf of Florida. We went loaded down with Harry's flies. And that meant that we had loads and loads of those extra-special ones Harry designs and ties himself. He had them on two boards, covered with strips of balsa wood, in which to stick the hooks. Harry really ties a showy fly for a showy fish—extra-good and extra-long saddle hackles for wings, tied on a 3/0 hook, some with chenille bodies and others without any bodies at all. The rest of the fly is dressed up with marabou feathers for more action, jungle cock feathers for eyes, a bit of red feather for shoulders—and how the tarpon love them! They looked very beautiful and as Harry handed them around, everyone dipped deeply and crammed them into their tackle boxes. Charlie put them in his hat and with the ones he already had there, he looked as if he would fly away at any minute.

We fished the waters out of Tavernier, two men and a guide to each skiff. That first morning as our guide, Rolie Hollenbeck, poled us out along the edge of a shallow lake, we immediately saw fish. My first cast brought a wicked strike. The fish hit the fly within 15 feet of the

134

boat and came leaping out right at us. And that was all! The fly sailed up in the air and Mr. 60-pound Tarpon "left out." Five minutes later, I spotted a smaller fish close to the surface. He hit with a bang and continued on up. This one was well hooked and after seven jumps and sixteen minutes of fight, I boated a 22-pounder. Within the next half-hour, I hooked and lost ten more fish.

After lunch we went out again and almost every fish I cast to, hit. In all, I must have had thirty fish on. Finally I put my streamer in front of a nice one and saw him take and plunge downward. I struck as hard as I dared, which was plenty, and for the next forty-two minutes was tied to a fighting silver king that knew all the tricks. I leaned back on the rod relentlessly the whole time and finally beat him, and when at last he was in the boat I was sure I had a world record. Since we were staying out on the cruiser that night, we put him away to weigh when we went ashore.

The next day, Charlie Ebbets, who is chief photographer of the *Miami News Bureau,* said that he wanted to take some pictures. "But just the same," he added jokingly, "I'm going to take my rod along. I might get a chance at a world-record fish."

Charlie didn't get any pictures that day. His first cast connected with a tarpon that put on the greatest display of aerial gymnastics I've ever seen. Charlie played him like a veteran. It took him fifty-five minutes to land the fish, and when we weighed him in that night, Charlie had his world record. It weighed an even 40 pounds, 2 pounds better than my catch of the day before!

For tarpon fishing, skiffs or light, shallow-draft craft

are used. The noise of a motor will frighten tarpon and the motor should be cut while you are still well out from the spot you want to fish. The silver king seems to scare more easily from an outboard motor than from a cruiser, because the cruiser's exhaust is above water while that of the outboard is below the surface.

The guide will pole you quietly into position, and once the fish is sighted, will stick the pole into the soft bottom and stake out while you make your casts. A good guide not only knows where the fish are, but can spot them easily while you are popping your eyes out vainly trying to see them.

I know all about that last statement, too. I went out with Frankee Albright to fish for tarpon in one of the lakes on the gulf side of the Keys. Frankee staked out on the edge and we waited. As I had forgotten my dark glasses, seeing fish was very tough indeed. Frankee didn't have glasses, either, but that did not bother her in the least. She could see fish that I couldn't, and when I had flushed several by casting blind in their general direction, I sat down and started thinking. Suddenly I had it. I stood up and waited for Frankee to spot a fish cruising by.

"There's one!" she cried.

I started to false cast, getting 30 feet of line up in the air and waving it back and forth. "Now, where is he?"

Frankee pointed. I put the line out 30 feet in that direction. "How much farther is he?" I asked.

"Twenty feet," she answered.

I cast and shot my line, stopping it at what I judged to be 15 feet of shoot.

"Is it close?" I asked.

"Right in front of him!" Frankee shouted. "Start stripping!"

He took, and came on out, 50 pounds of flashing silver, and tumbled back in, throwing water everywhere. Out he came again, and this time the fly flew high in the air.

We fished the rest of the afternoon in that manner, Frankee finding the fish, pointing out the direction to me and telling me how far to shoot my line. It worked, and although Frankee was a bit hoarse that night, she really did a job of remote-control fishing for me.

Another time I was fishing out of Marathon with Captain Elmo Capo. It was hot, and the middle of the day, and the fish were not moving. However, Elmo said that he knew a small opening in the mangroves where there were usually some fish. We eased up to the spot and didn't see a thing. Then I heard a faint blup from the direction of the mangroves.

"There they are," said Elmo.

I looked and looked but couldn't see any fish. Then I heard another blup.

"There, back under the mangroves," Elmo said. "Do you hear them?"

"What do you mean, 'hear them'?" I asked.

"That popping noise," he replied. "They burp and the air bubble comes to the surface and breaks. Stay quiet a while. They'll come out to see what's going on."

And sure enough, there they came, swimming slowly along in single file—a half-dozen fish that looked to be about 5 pounds apiece.

That experience has helped me to find tarpon many times since, and everytime I hear a tarpon burp I get a big kick out of it because when Elmo told me that the blupping noise I heard was a tarpon burping, he added, "Now listen closely, and you'll hear them say 'Pardon me.'"

Sometimes in the lakes you can spot rolling fish. You can follow their course as they swim around the shallow edges and often can take a short cut and pole across in front of them, and be set and ready for the cast as they approach. Strangely enough, you can stand up in a boat and cast and have a tarpon strike your lure even when it couldn't possibly help seeing you. One time I had a 100-pound tarpon come to my fly when it was within 5 feet of the boat. He came at it with his immense mouth wide open, ready to suck in the fly—and I struck! Of course, I pulled it right out of his mouth and I felt pretty foolish because I knew that you must wait until the fish has started down before striking. But the sight of that 100 pounds of tarpon roaring up in front of me was more than I could stand.

In spite of this apparent lack of fear, tarpon can be scared away, or at least downed, by fishing in the same spot too long. In one lake I know, far back in the mangroves and reached only after a long trip through overhanging branches, there are usually several schools of baby tarpon. When they are not cruising or rolling, you can do business with them in two spots on the lake. On the north end are two coves where the fish seem to lie when not on the move, and if you ease up on them quietly, you can generally have fun for about half an hour. Then they seem to realize that you mean danger and they stop hitting. But even at the beginning, if you get in too close,

138

they just refuse to hit. Many anglers are too careless in this way, and spoil their own chances of taking fish.

The fight of the big tarpon is spectacular to the *nth* degree—due mostly, of course, to his great leaping ability. But because of the flashiness of his leaps, enough has not been said about the fight he makes beneath the surface. The aerial acrobatics are nervewracking enough, I'll grant you, but when a 50-pound tarpon really gets into a fight, he is at his best down below. When such a tarpon takes off on a long run and you feel his tremendous power, you begin to realize the grueling battle ahead. Against a fly rod he is capable of runs ranging from 400 to 800 feet, and when a fish takes off like that, there is nothing to do but crank up the motor and go after him. You can save what line is left that way, and even recover a little, but what then? When he decides to go again, he will strip your reel—right now!

When he begins to tire, he will come to the top and roll. Those rolls are made in order to restore the fading supply of air and experienced guides claim that every time a tarpon rolls and gets a fresh supply, he is good for fifteen minutes more. And it does seem to work that way, as you can feel the renewed power every time he grabs some ozone. Fighting a fish like that is plenty tiring and before you are through, your arms and legs feel ready to fall off.

Strictly speaking, of course, tarpon from 50 to 150 pounds are not fly-rod fish. But there is a lot of fun in hooking such monsters even though you don't expect to or intend to land them. (Big tarpon can be landed, as witness Frankee Albright's 48½-pounder and Lee Cuddy's great fly-rod catch of a 63-pound silver king.)

The longest fight I ever had with any fish was a three-and-a-half-hour battle with what we estimated to be a 65-pound tarpon. He finally got away, though, and was as fresh when he departed as he was at the start of the fight. Needless to say, I was not!

Now, when I go for a big tarpon, I put an 8-pound test nylon leader on. When I get a fish securely hooked and have had the fun of the jumps, I point the rod at him and when the line straightens out, the leader breaks where it is tied onto the hook. I lose the fly but have more than its worth in fun.

But it is entirely possible to land a 100-pound fish if the angler is willing to stay with him and scrap it out. Naturally, some fish fight harder than others and if you are lucky enough to hook a tarpon in the gills, the battle is never so tough as when it is hooked in the mouth. This hooking in the gills is feasible because when a tarpon finds that the lure he has taken is artificial, he ejects it through the gills. So when I am trying for a big tarpon, I wait until I think he is throwing the fly through his gills, and then strike.

Once, when I was being guided by Frankee Albright, we got into a very large tarpon. When he took the fly, I waited while he went down a long way and then I struck as hard as I could. Out he came, throwing the water all over the place and looking to me like 200 pounds of fish! I let him run and jump and get over that first wild frenzy before bearing down on him. When he did ease up somewhat, I laid back on the rod and never gave him

Through the dark recesses of the Everglades in search of snook, channel bass, and tarpon. Passages like this one bore through the mangroves and open into lakes that hold untold numbers of hard-fighting fish. *Photo by Chas. C. Ebbets.*

Salt-water fly-fishing at its best. The results of a one-day encounter with tarpon and channel bass caught off Tavernier on the Florida Keys. Anglers (left to right): Joe Brooks, Charles Ebbets, Louis Mowbray of Bermuda, and Harry Friedman, with guides Holly and Rolie Hollenbeck. Fish: tarpon, 38 pounds, 22 pounds, 40 pounds; channel bass, 21 pounds, 22 pounds 8 ounces, and 23 pounds. *Photo by Chas. C. Ebbets.*

That great fly caster, Herbie Welch, of Maine, with the biggest bonefish ever caught on a fly. This 12-pound 4-ounce fish was caught off Islamorada while Herb was fishing with guide Jimmie Albright. *Photo by Chas. C. Ebbets.*

Ted Williams, one of baseball's all-time greats, is also a fine fly caster. He shows his first bonefish caught on a fly to the author. *Photo by Chas. C. Ebbets.*

a minute's rest. None of his subsequent runs was over 300 feet and while he jumped far and wide at first, his later leaps were halfhearted affairs. Sensing that he wasn't going to be too tough, I fought him boldly, and after half an hour told Frankee that he was mine.

"Don't be too sure," she said. "He looks like he's tiring fast, but you never know about tarpon."

In fifteen minutes more I had him on his side, 20 feet out from the skiff, dead beat. I started bringing him in, sliding him slowly along the surface.

"You have him in the gills," said Frankee. "He sure is beat!"

And just then the hook pulled out.

"He was about 85 pounds" was all Frankee said.

There was nothing to do but stand there and grin at each other. I thought of all the times I had hooked into big tarpon and fought them for hours, only to lose them. And now, with everything in my favor, and the fish hooked in the right place, the hook pulls out! I still feel that that was my fish.

So if you are seriously trying to land one of those big babies, remember to delay the strike. I have learned, too, that after the first mad effort to escape is over, you can pretty well judge whether or not you have a fair chance of landing the fish. There are some tarpon you tie into that are just plain wild fish against which you wouldn't have a chance if you used a derrick. That kind I break off in a hurry, before they break me. This, I might add, I only learned to do after losing three fly lines in quick succession to just such fish. Of course, I know that it is better to just stay away altogether from tarpon over 50 pounds when your weapon is a fly rod, but it's so much fun, and then, there's always hope. Now I hook my fish and then let him go during that first wild, frenzied rush and series of jumps, making no effort to tighten up on him. When he calms down, I put on all the pressure I can and never let up. The first of the three fly lines mentioned above went because I tightened up too much and the six-thread line I was using for backing just couldn't take it. On that fish I was using a 15-pound test leader, which was evidently stronger than the backing. Otherwise the leader would have broken first and I would have saved the line. The next reel I produced from my fishing bag had 10-pound test nylon casting line for backing. That baby didn't last any time at all and I watched the tarpon that had broken it off, leaping away in the distance trying to get rid of that $11 GAF Ashaway nylon line.

The next line I pulled from the tackle box had 12-pound test nylon casting line as backing. That lasted a bit longer but once more a big tarpon popped it! Now I use a 12-pound test nylon tippet on my tapered leader and my backing is 14-pound test nylon squidding line. That combination works very well indeed, and if anything goes it will be the tippet, in which case I lose only the fish, the fly, and part of the tippet.

The same kind of retrieve that is used for baby tarpon produces with the bigger fish and, oddly enough, the same lures are just as effective for the big boys. A 150-pound tarpon will hit a streamer fly 2 inches long and tied on a #2 hook. A popping bug of the same kind will produce results. However, if you are seriously trying to land one of those big fish, it pays to use a fly tied on a

#3/0 or 5/0 hook. It is also true that it is a bit harder to hook a tarpon on a popping bug than it is on a streamer. I believe that this is because when they suck the lure in, the floatability of the popper keeps it from going down as readily as a streamer fly would.

But the larger tarpon go for popping bugs in a big way. They will hit a slow or fast bring-back and they will hit the bug when it is lying motionless on the surface. If they seem a little temperamental in their reactions, a bit of experimenting will usually give you the answer. As a general rule, the slower retrieve is best, however.

Tarpon particularly tickle me in the way they react to a popping bug. It seems to arouse a playful streak in them and at times their performance will border on the ridiculous. Once, while using a white popper, I saw a 20-pound fish suddenly appear under it. He lay there for a moment, then began swimming around in circles, raising all the while until he came just under it. Then he butted it playfully with his nose, knocking it an inch or two out of water. I let it sit there and soon spied him again, still under the bug and looking sideways at it. He made a circle, came up, and slapped it with his tail. That time I struck, pulled the bug out of the water and then, after a false cast, dropped it back where it had been. Once again he began circling around it and seemed to keep turning his head all the time, as if to keep it in sight. I gave the bug a hard pop, and he left there in a hurry. But in a second he was back and this time he charged and I hooked him long enough to have two beautiful jumps.

However it is used, the popping bug does things to tarpon. It will attract them and bring them in close. I have

143

seen them, when swimming away, suddenly turn and come 20 feet to the hard pop of a bug. It will also locate them in lakes or other likely places where they are not in evidence but where you think they should be. Keep tossing the bug in and bringing it back in a series of loud, hard pops. Quite often this will stir them up and make them start to roll, and once having located them, you can cast to them with a fair assurance of a strike.

I had this well illustrated for me one day when I was fishing with Jimmie Albright. It was too cloudy to be able to spot cruising fish. We could see tarpon right enough, but they would appear so close to the boat that they would flush before I started to cast. So I put on a popper and started to cast blind. For ten minutes I popped away and then, about 60 feet off to the left I heard and saw two swirls. I looked back at the bug, which was then only 10 feet behind the boat, and as I looked, two tarpon came up under it, swimming in from my left. There was no doubt that the popper had interrupted their cruise and they had come over to see what it was all about. They didn't hit, but it certainly attracted them and later I had five hits, still while blind casting, and landed one 15-pound fish.

The popping bug is also by far the most effective weapon to use as dusk sets in, when tarpon cruise out into the shallow water to feed on night-running shrimp. They look for the shrimp in the channels back among the flats of the Gulf and even come out in numbers along the Overseas Highway and feed under the bridges where the current carries the shrimp through the spans. It is fun to fish for them at night from these bridges, but a fish hooked then is hard to land. Be sure to put a light tippet on the leader so that you can point the rod at the fish and break him off when you want to. Otherwise the tarpon may make one of his long runs and snap either your line or the backing where it is tied to the reel drum.

Such night angling puts the final fascination in tarpon fishing. The water is usually glassy and when tarpon begin to roll all around you, you can't decide which way to cast. In the failing light the ripples where fish have showed glint silver and gold, and everything is muted and mysterious. Then a tarpon hits your popper and comes out shaking his head and throwing water all about, gill covers extended and gill rakers clattering, and your heart does a rhumba beat that sets your ears ringing and fogs your eyes. And just when your head clears and you begin to breathe normally, you see your fly tossed skyward and catch the last derisive flip of the tarpon's tail, and then hear the resounding splash of cold water. There goes the silver king!

Tarpon like popping bugs and they like them played slowly. They like plenty of time to look the lure over and a fast retrieve usually takes it away from them. Give a tarpon a chance to make up his mind and he will hit it almost every time.

The streamers tied on 3/0 hooks with 4½-inch feathers are best for tarpon from 20 pounds up, while the smaller silver kings fancy the streamers tied on the smaller, 1/0 hooks. And with tarpon, the white-wing streamer with red hackle and the yellow-wing with red hackle seem by far the best patterns for either large or small fish. They will hit other color combinations, but not so readily.

9.

Snook

THE snook that is found in American waters is named from the Dutch word *snoek,* meaning pike. In some parts of his habitat he is also called *robalo,* derived from the Spanish name for bass. So Mr. Snook is named in two different countries for his two most outstanding characteristics—snook because he looks like a pike and *robalo* because he acts like a largemouth black bass. The body is silver sided with a tinge of brown, and the snout is indeed pikelike. But the most noticeable feature is the strongly marked lateral line. Technically speaking, he is *Centropomus undecimalis,* and has a range from the West Indies north to Florida, throughout Puerto Rico, and is very common in the Gulf of Mexico.

Snook are plentiful in nearly all canals, bays, rivers, and estuaries throughout Florida and many outstanding catches of large specimens are made in such much-used waters as Biscayne Bay, where anglers fish for them from the bridges of Miami and Miami Beach as well as from boats. They also reach great numbers along the southwestern portion of the state and one of the greatest concentration points is in the Ten Thousand Islands section.

The snook is a vicious hitter to a fly or surface lure, a strong, dogged fighter, and he frequently takes to the air. His feeding, which is mainly upon minnows, is accomplished with loud strikes and splashes as he herds schools of fry into the banks and feeds upon them. He also likes crabs and shrimp.

However, the snook himself leads a somewhat harried life. Near most large communities the commercial netters take terrific toll, and even far back in the Everglades, as the fish work up a lateral canal on the incoming tide, a family living back there will stretch chicken wire across the canal and when the tide drops the whole family will wade in with clubs and go to work. They gather in the clubbed fish, put aside those they want for themselves, and then carry off the rest and sell them.

You fish for snook very much as you do for largemouth bass, slowly, and with many casts back to the same spot. Cast the streamer in as close to the mangroves as you can, let it sink about a foot, then use a very slow retrieve. Be sure to let it sink. This is so important that many fly tiers are making weighted flies for snook. Use slow, foot-long jerks, speeding it up as the fly nears you. It needs a lot of coaxing to bring them out of their resting places under the mangroves and sometimes they will follow quite a way before taking. But when a snook does come out, he rushes in savagely and knocks your lure for a loop. His fight is strong and powerful and marked by constant boring back toward the shelter of the mangroves. When you do get him into clear water, he takes to the air and more often than not manages to land on the wrong side of a mangrove root, with disastrous results for the angler. To

148

add to all these hazards, he has further trouble for the fisherman in the form of a sharp plate on his gill cover—an ideal weapon for cutting your leader in no time flat. And when I say sharp, I mean be careful. It's sharp enough to put a bad gash on your fingers if you handle him carelessly.

Most of the lures that are popular with snook fishermen are best played slowly. When using a popper, let it stay still for almost half a minute after it hits the water. Pop it, and then let it sit there again for the same length of time. Another pop, another rest period, then bring it back slowly, popping it until you are ready to pick it up for the next cast. Often they will hit the bug as it lies still on the surface.

Don't worry about making noise with the bug. Snook like it that way.

A wounded minnow lure should also be played slowly. This lure half-rolls and dives and generally performs a very good imitation of the real thing. It will take plenty of fish and it has been my experience that when snook do not respond too well to a popper or a streamer, they go in a big way for the wounded minnow. They like big streamers, too, tied with the saddle hackle flared outward—the breather type of fly on which the feathers come together as you make your strip, and "breathe" outward as you stop. The same theory applies in the case of the tail feathers on poppers and wounded minnows and there is no doubt about the efficiency of lures tied in this manner. They take a lot of snook.

In April of 1949, Harry Friedman, Jack Knight, Charlie Ebbets, and I went on a two-day trip in the Ten Thousand

Islands section of the Everglades—object, snook. We left the Rod and Gun Club dock at Everglades City in the evening, aboard the *Snooky,* with Captain Bob Thompson, and cruised toward the fishing grounds until midnight. We then anchored and the next morning took to skiffs with outboards and went speeding back through channels in the dense mangrove stands to some beautiful-looking water.

I had some of my yellow popping bugs along and started off using those. I'd drop the bug at the edge of the mangroves, let it sit still on the water for half a minute, then give it a pop. They started hitting that bug at once. They hit it when it was floating still on top, when it was being retrieved slowly, and when I brought it back fast. Fishing in the same skiff with me, Jack Knight used a streamer and did just as well. In the second skiff we could see the other boys far down the shore line, also very busy catching fish.

Those snook kept socking my bug for about half an hour, and then went down. Jack continued to take them on streamers, so it wasn't long before I tied one on, too, and started doing business again. Then, late in the afternoon, when the shadows started creeping along the mangroves, I put my yellow popper back on and once again had surface action. But during the hot part of the day, you might as well have offered them banana splits on top. They just weren't interested.

Nearly every fish I landed on that trip roughed the leader tippet so badly that I would have to tie on another one. Many of them cut it right through. I don't like to use

150

wire on the end of my leader but wire would have saved some fish, flies, and tippets.

In southern Florida, the snook begin to come into the canals in March. Fish from 5 to 20 pounds make into the canals along the Tamiami Trail, moving up from the gulf on an incoming tide. Around the first of May, more small snook come in and together with the March fish, stay until August, go back out, and then make another visit in September. On the whole, the best fishing is in May, June, and July. A lot of the bigger snook stay in the canals all year, feeding heavily on minnows and frogs, and the really big fish of 20 pounds and up seem to go out only about once a year. They are content to take it easy in the canals where food is plentiful and not too hard to secure. It tells in their fight, too. A snook that has been in the canals a while does not begin to wage the fight that one of the same size puts up out in the gulf, and the latter are also much brighter-looking fish.

One day when I was fishing in the Gulf near Tavernier with Rolie Hollenbeck, I saw a school of silvery fish darting by. I put a fly in front of them and came up with a very nice snook. He fought hard and it was quite a while before Rolie slipped the net under him. He weighed about 10 pounds and was almost as silvery as a bonefish. Later we spotted other snook in that bay and tarried long enough to do battle with and land eight of them. They were all about the same size and all were in excellent condition.

Snook spawn in the shallow grasses back from the canals. The eggs hatch out and the fry stick around until they are about 2½ or 3 inches long, then move slowly through and out of the brackish waters of the canals, into the salt.

Temperatures seem to affect snook to quite an extent. When the water drops below 65 degrees, they go down and just aren't interested in your lures. And in southern Florida, a northwest wind puts them down. The best temperature is between 75 and 80 degrees, at which time the snook will hit on top, as well as immediately below the surface.

An effective way to take snook when they are not coming too good, is to draw them out for a look at a popper, then tie on a streamer. Usually when they show enough interest to look at the surface lure, but don't quite have the urge to sock it, they will hit a streamer hard.

Snook fishing is probably better at dawn and just before dark and there is no question that nighttime is just about the best time of all to go for this species. Personally, I don't like to fish at night, but for those who do, a sally out for snook will certainly bring results.

One afternoon in 1949, I went out along the Tamiami Trail with Fausto Nieva, who has been fishing that road for years. Fausto had a lot of dope on the snook migrations and also knew some of the hot spots just off the Trail, but still hard enough to get to that they were not overfished. Best of all, he knew the time of year to look for them in those spots. A week one way or the other, and the fish just wouldn't be there.

Reports had been trickling in as to 15- and 20-pound snook being caught on the trail and just two days before, Fausto himself had landed a 12-pounder. As we drove along, he pointed out good snook water and told me just what stretches were good at certain times. I wrote it all carefully down and cashed in on it later. But that day we kept on going, heading for Bridge Number 73. We finally reached it, pulled off to the side of the road, and put up our tackle to start fishing.

"Look at that strike!" Fausto suddenly shouted.

I looked up the canal and saw the diminishing waves of what had evidently been the swirl of a huge fish.

"Take this fly," Fausto said, handing me a large yellow fly. It felt a bit heavy as I juggled it in my hand, and he told me that it was weighted, to get it down deep. I tied it on, and running up to where the big swirl had occurred, started to cast. I let it sink until it was out of sight and then began the retrieve. On the second strip I felt as if I had hooked a manatee. My rod tip shot down and everything stopped. Then I spied a great shape down in the water and as I watched, it seemed as if the whole bottom was moving off down the canal. Then he came up on top and swirled. He looked so big that I felt like jumping in after him. But he had decided he wanted out, and off he went down the canal, with me following after him as best I could, still losing line as we went. As I passed Fausto he was shouting advice to me, but I tore over the bridge, too busy to hear him, and went on down the canal.

Several passing cars slowed up and one stopped just as the snook came half out of the water. I heard a muttered exclamation from the direction of the car, heard a grind of gears, and then the diminishing roar of the motor in the distance. That driver didn't want any part of such a fish!

From the shouts and chattering behind me, I knew that Fausto was still machine-gunning advice. But what more could I do? I was hanging on, leaning back on the rod, and catfooting it along after that fish. And so far, the snook wasn't even puffing.

And then, suddenly the hook shot into the air. I saw the casual flip of a caudal fin and heard a great groan from Fausto.

When I got back to where my fishing companion was continuing to put his tackle together, he merely hunched his shoulders, as if to say, "Well—that's fishing."

As I prepared to cast where another snook had broken water, I muttered hopefully that that fish must have weighed 30 pounds.

Fausto, who should know, brought me back to earth.

"No, only about twenty," he allowed. "But a very nice fish."

It is generally useless to fish for snook with any other than a breather-type fly. At times they will hit a bucktail or a spinner-bucktail combination, but on the whole they like a lure with plenty of action to the feathers. If played correctly, the breather-type streamers never stop moving —the motion is there and is always a temptation to any snook that spots the lure. The streamers should at all times be allowed to sink at least a foot before the retrieve is begun, and then the bring-back should start in long, slow strips, gradually increasing in speed until the lure is picked up for the next cast. It's different, of course, if you spot a traveling school out in open water. Then a quick toss and a fairly fast retrieve pays off. But for consistent strikes, your streamers must get down to the fish, which, basslike, are slow and need coaxing, particularly during the heat of the day. Repeated casts to the same spot help. The snook is more like a largemouth bass in its reactions to a fly-rod lure than any other fish I know of.

Poppers are a great snook lure, too, and are usually at their best around dawn and up until about eight A.M. (although now and again, they will be terrific all day long). From five P.M. until dark, snook will once again rise to the popper, and if you fish at night, a popper is the thing!

10.

The Spotted Sea Trout,
The Sea Trout

THE spotted sea trout found along the eastern seaboard carries a wide variety of names. In the books he is *Cynoscion nebulosis.* In the south he is the spotted sea trout. Throughout the Carolinas, Virginia, and parts of Maryland he is the spotted squeteague, and from there on up to New York he is commonly named the spotted weakfish. In the list of names of salt-water game fish compiled by the Outdoor Writers Association of America, both "spotted sea trout" and "spotted weakfish" are used.

While his official distribution is from New York to Texas, he is most common along the southern part of his habitat and becomes somewhat rare north of Virginia. He seems to be at his best in the shallow Florida waters and reaches a peak in the Gulf of Florida, where he is found in great numbers. Since the spotted sea trout is fished for commercially in that area, the ranks are dwindling somewhat each year and it is to be hoped that it will not be too long before legislation is enacted to stop the wholesale thinning of this fine game fish.

Spotted sea trout are willing takers of fly-rod lures and make plenty of good angling because they come into the shallow water in schools and range over the grassy flats, cruise the channels, and scatter far and wide in bays and estuaries and at times along the jetties of the ocean.

Practically all fly-fishing for the spotted sea trout is from a boat, but there are places and times when it can be done from the shore. You can wade the shallow edges of channels and occasionally get out into the shallow bays to put a lure in front of them.

They like flashy colors in streamers and they also like the sparkle of a spinner in front of a streamer. When the water temperature is right, they go all out for a hard-popped bug. In fact, the louder the pop, the better the results, usually. Commercial fishermen after these fish in the gulf, use a big cork which they pop hard to attract the fish and bring them to the bait.

When wading, a longer cast may be necessary, but generally speaking a throw of 40 feet is enough. And the speed of the retrieve doesn't seem to matter. Sometimes they like a slow bring-back and at other times they will go for a fast one. A bit of experimenting will soon tell you their mood of the moment.

One April, I fished with Bill Mann of Miami, out of Flamingo in the Cape Sable area of southern Florida. Bill is a hot trout fisherman and knows every Key and flat in that wonderful fishing territory. He uses a two-handed plug rod and a wide variety of plugs, most of which are red and white, or red and yellow, or a mixture of those colors. On this trip he used surface plugs very effectively, bringing the fish charging for his lure out of places where they just weren't supposed to be. It was a revelation to me.

We had two days of it and went through all manner of

158

experiences. It blew a gale, almost, both days, and though it was tough fly casting, I stuck to my fly rod, using streamers and poppers, and managed to do all right. Gales, storms, typhoons—nothing seemed to bother Bill. He'd throw out that plug, which he calls his "worm," bring it back with plenty of action, and haul in trout, right and left. And all the time he was smoking a big black cigar and talking a blue streak.

"Now Joe," he'd say, "I'll throw out my worm and you watch what happens."

It would happen, all right. Bill was certainly hitting on all six. And although it was certainly fishing under the worst of fly-rod conditions, I wasn't suffering, either. Apparently nothing could stop those fish from making excursions to the surface with the sole intent of knocking the feathers off those cork foolers. I would toss the popper out, give it the hardest pop I could, then let it sit for a moment, then bring it back in a series of slow pops. They fell all over it, some of the smaller ones coming clear out of the water as they struck. Sometimes they took the bug on the way up and when I pulled back on my rod while they were still in the air, it sent them tumbling. At other times, their habit of following the bug in almost to the boat before they struck would catch me with my rod way up in the air, struggling to keep a tight line and set the hook at the same time. We didn't get many big fish that trip, but we did take some around 4 pounds and certainly had plenty of fun.

But like most fish, spotted sea trout have their days to be selective, too. Ed Pacetti of Homestead, was fly-fishing Barnes Sound with a friend. Things were very slow until at last, after repeated changes of lure, Ed put on an Upperman Streamer with white wings, white body, and red hackle at the throat. It was tied on a 3/0 Z nickle hook, giving it the weight he figured it needed to get the fly down to where the fish were. While his fellow angler searched frantically through his fly box for a similar lure, Ed caught sixteen spotted sea trout, the largest a bit under 5 pounds. Then, since it was the only such fly they had, Ed turned the rod over to the other fellow and watched him land several nice fish.

During the period of no activity, they had tried at least fifteen different flies, although Ed still feels that if they had been tied on 3/0 hooks, they might have done well, too. At any rate, spotted sea trout sure do like a red-and-white, or a red-and-yellow mixture far better than any other color combination.

Like so many other species, the larger spotted sea trout —weighing from 8 to 10 or 11 pounds—seem to like to range the channels alone. You don't get so many of those big fellows, but they are around and there's always hope. They like a big long streamer with a spinner in front of it. Long casts seem best, too, giving you coverage of lots of water and allowing you to make long retrieves, which in turn give the old lunkers plenty of space in which to look the lure over. When a big spotted sea trout swirls back of your lure, he gives you a shock. He makes one of those gigantic boils that are seen mostly in dreams. There is no doubt about it having been a big fish.

On the Indian River, near Melbourne, Florida, Dick Splaine has been fishing for spotted sea trout for years. He worked for a long time developing a fly especially for the larger ones, and has brought his invention to its present efficiency only after years of experimenting. During one phase of the evolution of the big streamer, he was missing a lot of strikes. He finally noticed that the fish were hitting up at the head of the fly, and his next step was the addition of a free-swinging head hook. Right away those missed strikes were corrected and eight of the next ten trout he landed were caught on that newly added hook.

Dick likes to go after the big spotted sea trout in the channel along the causeway just east of the town of Melbourne, and there he has landed some which weighed 9 and 10 pounds.

Early one spring I went from Miami up to Melbourne to join Dick in some fishing. Just before I left, I had been out in the gulf and had a good day's fishing for spotted sea trout with poppers. They took readily and I left the popper on all day.

But it was colder at Melbourne, and after half an hour of futile casting, and of watching Dick pull them in on his streamer, I agreed with Dick that the water was just too cold for surface lures. Dick had noticed the effect of temperature on the fish before, too, and said that he would try the poppers later when the weather had warmed up a bit. Three weeks later I had a letter from him saying that he and his wife were both taking plenty of nice spotted sea trout on poppers.

Incidentally, while I was writing the above—October, 1949—along came another letter from Dick to tell me that his wife had just taken a 9-pound fish on a popper. He also added that when he and Mrs. Splaine first started fly-fishing for spotted sea trout at Melbourne, they were

161

the only ones using fly equipment. Now he says he knows of at least fifty anglers who go out with the fly rod in that area.

SEA TROUT

One of the most popular fish along such northern shores as the New Jersey coast and Long Island is the sea trout. His range is from Massachusetts Bay down along the eastern seaboard to the east coast of Florida, and throughout his range he furnishes sport for thousands of anglers.

Cynoscion regalis, as he is formally known, is so numerous that large catches are the rule rather than the exception. They are called "tide runners" in some places and there are many tales of the enormous schools that race the beaches, coming in mostly at night. They will hit flies and poppers and when you find a school of them and can stay with them, you will have all the action you want. Charter-boat captains who take parties out to fish for sea trout are a little inclined to frown on the fly rodder, for when he ties into a fish, all the other anglers in the boat have to take in their trolling lines until he lands it. You don't bring in the sea trout in a few minutes on such light tackle.

In the fall the sea trout move into estuaries and bays and in such places frequently furnish great fly-rod fishing to anglers who walk the salty marshes and cast into the nearby water. The fish work the banks in search of food and you may come up with anything from a 2- to a 10-pounder. In that shallow water, poppers seem to attract

162

the fish and there is no hesitancy in their strike. They fall all over it.

They are usually in at such spots as Barnegat Inlet, in September and October, and those 6- to 12-pound fighters like nothing better than to knock the dressing off a yellow streamer or popper.

At Round About Bay, the mouth of the Mullica River, twelve miles north of Atlantic City, Morrie Upperman and I had some fine popper fishing for the larger trout. The tide was high, and there was about 3 feet of water at the edge of the marsh. Boils and swirls showed where the sea trout were cruising. Single fish work through there, and as usual, they were bigger than the school fish. Morrie's first cast brought a strike and I watched him struggling with what later proved to be a 6-pounder. The fish walloped that yellow popper with such a noise that it made me jump. But I didn't do much watching. I was soon hooked into a slightly smaller fish and from then on we had plenty of action. Stripers also work in that water and we landed several of those, weighing about 3 pounds apiece, as well as the sea trout. One striper that slapped at Morrie's bug looked as if he might have gone 10 pounds. He didn't come back, though, and then we were into a school of sea trout. This time they were smaller, around 2 and 3 pounds, and we each took several before they went down. Then, at dusk, bigger fish moved in again, and we had all the excitement we wanted from there on out.

When fishing from a boat, casts into the rocks along inlets will often pick up some big sea trout, and where you can walk out on sandy bars and fish the tidal current as it sweeps in or out of a bay, you can occasionally find a school working. On grassy flats, be sure to make a cast to any sandy holes you see amid the grass. Sea trout frequent such spots and a well-placed cast will often bring a strike. The best water depth seems to be about 3 to 8 feet. If the water is any deeper than that, they seldom rise to a fly.

The same retrieve as is used for the spotted sea trout will get results with the sea trout. Be sure to play the lure right in close, too, because like his cousin, he has a habit of following a long way before hitting. And with a popping bug, use plenty of action. They like a lot of noise and a lot of water commotion.

The sea trout and the spotted sea trout like the same lures. They go for a yellow popper tied on a 3/0 hook, and they like it best with plenty of noise. The harder you pop it, the better. In streamers they prefer the larger size, with 4½-inch feathers, and they like yellow better than other colors, with white running a close second.

11.

Channel Bass

THE channel bass, *Sciaenops ocellatus*, also called the red drum and redfish, is probably best known to the masses of anglers as the favorite of surf casters. When found in suitable water, it is also a very fine game fish for lighter tackle.

Its range is from New York to Texas, with the largest specimen occurring in the coastal waters of North Carolina, Virginia, Maryland, and Delaware. In these states, catches of fish weighing from 45 to 50 pounds are not uncommon. The world record is somewhere around 85 pounds. But the majority of fly-rod catches of the species have been made in Florida waters where the redfish, which is the popular name there, use the same flats as bonefish in the Bay of Florida, and are also found on the ocean side of the Keys. The hot spot for them seems to be back on the gulf side of the Keys and throughout the Ten Thousand Island section of the Everglades. Some few are taken from West Lake on the Flamingo Road while casting from the shore, and now and then you find some in the canals. But to catch them consistently, you must take a boat and

165

head out from shore, fishing the shallow waters and flats surrounding the numerous Keys that dot the gulf.

The channel bass in this area do not grow to large size, or, possibly, when they do reach a weight much above 25 pounds, they may migrate to deeper water. It is possible that they then journey up the coast and join the schools of larger fish in the coastwise movement that brings out so many surf casters. At any rate, until very recently the fly-rod unofficial record for channel bass was a 24-pound, 6-ounce catch made by Red Greb of Miami. The fish was 41½ inches long and had a girth of 21½ inches. Then in 1949, Lee Cuddy, also of Miami, posted a 25-pound channel bass for top place on a fly rod, and as far as I know, that one still holds.

It has only been during the past three or four years that any numbers of anglers have been fly casting for channel bass, but now they get a big play. They are an all-year-round fish but seem to be in the shallows in greater numbers, and in greater sizes in the early spring and throughout the summer.

Most of the fly-fishing for the species is done from a boat. Poling over the flats gives you an excellent chance to spot the bass when they are tailing, and when they are in schools they can be located by the red color they give to the water where they lie.

Channel bass have a habit of swimming along, then stopping and, if they have seen you, hiding in the grass. They are good at the game, and very hard to locate again, but when they do that, it pays to stick around. Many a time I have searched for those hiding fish, become discouraged and started on, only to have them flush prac-

166

tically right under the boat. This habit of stopping has one advantage, in that it gives you added casts and will give you chances at more fish. When a bass spots you as he swims by, keep right on casting to him. Sometimes, when he gets out of range, you can follow him and catch up and still take him. In the shallow water of the flats, you can trace them by the wave of water they shove up in front of them as they move along.

When you see a single fish swimming by, try for a cast right on his nose. If he doesn't take, cast again and time it so your fly or popper crosses immediately in front of him. Hold the strike, for the channel bass is usually a slow taker.

I remember a day when I was fishing with Jack Ardis and Allen Corson. We went out from Tavernier on the Florida Keys, with Rolie and Hollie Hollenbeck guiding. They lost no time in finding fish for us, and the first one to which I cast took the popper, and the fight was on. He weighed about 5 pounds.

A little later, Rolie pointed out another one. It was lying still in a big sandy hole in the grass. I had a streamer on then, because we were working shallower water and I knew that in such water the pop of a bug might frighten them. I cast the streamer about 10 feet beyond and to the left of the fish and started to strip in the line. "Old red" didn't move, even though the fly seemed close enough for him to see it.

"Drop it on his nose," Jack advised. "They don't see well."

This time I put the fly about a foot in front of him. I

saw his big mouth open and I struck, hard—and the fly came shooting up into the air.

I turned to Jack. "I hit in time, didn't I?" I asked.

"It's not that," he answered. "As a matter of fact, you hit too soon. They suck the fly in and you didn't give him time. You pulled it right out of his mouth."

After that I gave them plenty of time, even going so far as to wait until I felt the fish, before striking. So with channel bass, always remember these two things: drop the fly right on their noses, and delay your strike.

The fight of the channel bass up to 25 pounds in weight is not a spectacular one as they do not jump and seldom make runs of more than 100 feet. But they hit hard and have a lot of power. They have a trick of shaking their heads viciously from side to side and nosing into the bottom and rubbing their jaws back and forth in the mud in an effort to dislodge the hook. And occasionally you run into a really tough one. I remember one trip, in particular, with Jimmie Albright, when I hooked a fish that went through all the tricks for me, shaking his head, digging his nose in the bottom, boring into the grass. Once, when he dug his nose into the mud, his big tail came straight up and I pulled back on the rod and turned him completely over. Then I had him coming and finally dragged him into the net. Jimmie hauled him aboard, took the hook out, and put him back. He looked like an 8-pound fish and fought like a 15-pounder.

On another trip back into the gulf out of Tavernier, Charlie Ebbets, Harry Friedman, Louis Mowbray, and I had some of the best channel-bass fishing I've ever been in on. We used poppers and streamers and we had a hit from almost every fish we cast to. Several times both boats had fish on at the same time. We took a lot that weighed between 5 and 10 pounds and the biggest ran 18½, 19, 21, and 22½, the last four being a bit larger, I would say, than the average bass in those waters. It was the kind of fishing that every angler wants to get into, when he goes out for channel bass—but that only happens once in a long time.

Channel bass will hit a streamer a bit quicker than they will hit a popping bug. They like the poppers well enough when you are fishing for them in the deeper water —from 4 to 6 feet deep—but when the big reds are feeding on the shallow banks, they shy from the popper most of the time and even with streamers you must creep up on them, and present the fly with delicacy. Yet channel bass are a funny fish with a fly. Often you can follow them as they cruise through the shallow water, spotting them by the wave they push in front of them, and if you keep casting in front of their noses, they will frequently hit.

They like yellow in both streamers and bugs, and also go for the red hackle and white feather combination or just a plain white popper. But the one thing to always remember in casting a fly or any other lure to a channel bass is to put it right smack in front of his big wide mouth. Because they don't see a bit well, and unless you put the lure where they can't possibly miss seeing it, you will not have the hits.

12.

Ladyfish

On the Indian River near Vero Beach, Dick Splaine and I were having some exciting sport with spotted sea trout. We were taking trout that weighed 3 and 4 pounds, and which seemed to like nothing better than to follow our streamers practically in to our feet before hitting. Suddenly I heard a shout from Dick and looking around, saw his rod bent down to the water. About 100 feet out, a long, slender, silvery fish came out and in and out again in a flash.

"Ladyfish!" I thought. "You can't mistake those jumping jacks!"

As I watched, Dick's line went slack and he called out that the fish was off. I made ready for a cast, but before I could get it away, there was another shout from Dick.

"Another one hit while I was bringing the line in!" he cried.

Then I heard a splash near me and saw the water disturbance. I chucked my popper out that way and immediately had a strike. "We're in a school of them," I said. "This is going to be good."

And for the next fifteen minutes, until the school moved on, we had fast and furious action.

The ladyfish is a long, silver, transparent-looking fish with big black eyes. It is often called "10-pounder" and "chiro," and on the west coast of Florida has erroneously been termed "bonefish." However, there should be no difficulty in identifying these two species correctly. They do not look alike and anyone who has fished for both lady-fish and bonefish knows that each one puts up a characteristic fight. The ladyfish carries on a great deal of the struggle in the air, while the bonefish never jumps. Nevertheless, because of existing confusion in nomenclature, the best way to designate the species you mean is to use the scientific name of *Albula vulpes* for the bonefish and *Elops sauris* for the ladyfish.

The ladyfish travels in schools over most of the warm seas. It is found around the Florida Keys, in the Gulf of Florida, and along the Atlantic Coast. Its northern range more or less ends in North Carolina, although there are records of ladyfish being taken in Massachusetts. The Pacific ladyfish does not go north of the Gulf of California but in that western ocean, and particularly around Hawaii, they grow to much greater size than their eastern cousins.

In Florida ladyfish cover a lot of ground. They cruise the inlets and bays, range the ocean, scatter wide over shallow, grassy beds, and lurk in the bisecting channels waiting for food to come to them. They do not move about much in the daytime, but as dusk approaches they come out of their resting places and start to feed. They work the channels hard, feeding on shrimp that float or swim by and on small crabs and minnows. When they strike their prey on top of the water, the sharp sound they make carries a long way. They put on an exhibition of fast and fancy feeding until their appetites are sated.

While the best angling time for ladyfish is at night, they can be taken in the daylight hours, too. You don't begin to do so well as when they are definitely on the feed, but every now and again you can entice one out to make a pass at your lure. And ever so often you may find a daytime school on the prod and as long as you can stay with them, you will have action. But for consistent sport with ladyfish, the pay-off hours are early morning, dusk, and during the night.

Ladyfish are sprinters rather than runners. They are just about the fastest-moving fish I have ever seen, coming out of the water and in again and out again so fast that they remind me of a weasel poking his head out of a stump—so fast that you think there must be several of them in there. Their short dashes, quick turns, and flashing leaps are like lightning. They will jump 5 feet away from you, hit the water, and leap right back again. They are so fast that it is impossible to keep a tight line. At the strike, you set the hook and then hang on as best you can until the fish has tired himself out with his frantic efforts to escape. After that you can catch up on your slack and finally bring him in.

The strike of this species is hard and fast. You don't hook a great many of them, and after they have been hooked their jumping ability makes them difficult to land because in addition to being one of the quickest fish I have ever seen, they pack a lot of power and know how to use it. I've never taken one that weighed more than 3 pounds, but those lucky anglers who have tied into ladyfish that weighed 4 and 5 pounds say that they are just about as much fish as you want to handle.

Although they will hit streamers and bucktails, too, my best luck in taking ladyfish has been with a popper, using a very fast retrieve. On all lures they go for a fast bring-back and they like them played on top or just under the surface. I prefer the popper because I like to see and hear the strike and because it seems to me that their surface strike packs more power.

The most exciting ladyfishing I ever remember was also my first encounter with the species. Allen Corson, fishing editor of the *Miami Herald*, asked me if I would like to do a bit of night fishing from the bridges around the cities of Miami and Miami Beach. The vagaries of the tide result in different fishing conditions at each one and like a great many Miamians, Allen knows just the right time to fish each bridge for ladyfish.

On this particular night we took off for the MacArthur Causeway.

"We should hit the incoming tide just right," Allen said as we walked out on the bridge.

Anglers hung over the railings, using rods of every description, and mostly fishing with bait. We passed the majority of them and then, about a quarter of the way out, Allen stopped and looked over the side. Thirty feet off, we saw and heard a splash, then another farther out, and to add the finishing touch, one exploded right under us.

"They're in!" Allen said. "Cast, and you should have some action."

174

With all those fish surfacing right under my nose, I already had my line in the air. Cars were whizzing by behind me, but I was not going to be beaten by that—fish were breaking!

We were about 20 feet above the water and I realized that it would be tough to play the popping bug I had tied on my leader. But I held the rod way down, with the tip pointing at the water, and started popping. After the fifth pop, a streak of silver, brought out by the bridge lights, showed clearly behind the lure. It zoomed up like a flash of lightning and dealt the bug a ferocious blow. I struck too late.

With one eye on the roadway to see that I didn't hang a passing automobile, I heaved the bug out again and this time had a hit almost immediately. I hooked him and then was treated to that vivid display of acrobatics so characteristic of the ladyfish. Such jumping I never did see! But finally I played him out, brought him in under me, grasped the line and leader, and hand-lined the fish up. I looked with admiration at that 2 pounds of ladyfish, then took the hook out and dropped him back into the water as gently as I could.

Strikes came for another half hour, and then Allen said that the tide was wrong and off we went, headed for a bridge at Miami Beach where he said conditions should be right. This time we crept through someone's backyard, groped our way down a bank, and eased out onto a narrow bit of land at the foot of the bridge. We heard fish as we neared the water and from a distance could see the splash as they broke. As soon as we offered our lures, they hit, and again we had fast and furious action for a half hour. Then things slowed up again.

"Hurry!" cried Allen. "I know another bridge."

By this time, of course, I was on to the procedure. You dash madly from one bridge to another to catch the tide just right, fish furiously for half an hour, rush to the car and nip off again for the next span.

I don't remember what bridge we were standing on when I glanced guiltily at my wristwatch. It was four ten.

"Four ten . . . that's A.M.," I thought. "Ye gods!"

"How about a sandwich?" I ventured. "It's getting late."

"Well," agreed Allen, "if you're hungry, we might as well eat."

"And," I continued, after we had hied ourselves to an all-night eatery, "I believe that I am getting sleepy. Do you think we could call it a day?"

So we went home then, but I knew that Allen was thinking, "And all the time, I thought that guy liked to fish."

Ladyfish like white poppers tied on 3/0 hooks and white bucktails tied on 1/0 hooks. They like those lures fished fast, along the top of the water. When feeding on shrimp floating with the tide, they strike them hard on top or just below the surface of the water, and so it is with the artificial lures. Impart to the popper a 6-inch jerk, accompanied with a loud pop, and give the same length jerk and a still faster retrieve to the white bucktail. And be sure to sharpen the hook before going for that elusive, fast, acrobatic silver streak. Strike at the flash, and strike hard, for they are difficult to hook and are so quick that a moment's hesitation will enable them to toss the hook.

13.

Barracuda

GREAT barracuda, scientifically named *Sphyraena barracuda*, are very numerous in southern waters and seem to travel up the Atlantic Coast to South Carolina, and now and again even show as far north as Massachusetts. They are particularly accessible to fly rodders in Florida waters, where they are found in almost every setting—in channels, shallow bays, and lakes. On the gulf side of the Keys, at low tide you sometimes see cudas that weigh 8, 10, and 12 pounds lying in the shallow water as motionless as logs. On the ocean side, they are numerous along the deep edge of the flats, either lying there quietly, or cruising slowly along like miniature submarines. Out there they often go as high as 30 and 40 pounds. The smaller ones hang around the edges of the mangroves and patrol the channels, and they also like to cruise over the grass beds on the deeper flats.

The same species is also common in the waters surrounding the island of Bermuda.

They are fierce, vicious, hard-hitting fish that show great speed for short distances and make some amazing leaps when hooked on a fly. From a fly-rod standpoint,

177

they can also cause a lot of grief on account of their habit of hitting the fly up near the head and cutting the leader in nothing flat. The best way to beat this hazard is to tie 6 inches of wire on the end of the leader. This is strong enough to stand the snap of those razorlike teeth and long enough to protect the leader. Number 2 wire is thin and does not interfere too much with the action of the fly when you are casting. But, as many tournament rules call for a leader material which does not test more than 15 pounds, it is best to try the breaking strength of the wire. If you are not interested in tournaments or world records, it doesn't matter, and # 2 wire will serve very well.

If you don't resort to wire, you may be in for a lot of trouble as sometimes you will encounter a school of small barracuda that will hit the lure everytime it comes close to them. Sometimes when you are fishing the flats, and casting blind, they will rob you of every fly you own. To overcome this and still avoid using wire, Red Greb started to make barracuda flies with the dressing tied well back on the bend of the hook. This left the shank clear back to the eye, free of feathers. The fly worked fairly well, serving as a foil for the sharp teeth of the cuda, but even so, the long-snouted fish would often clamp down on the leader.

Their teeth are terrible weapons. They slot together when the jaws close and if a finger happened to be in the way, it would be just too bad. The dispatch with which they can cut a small fish in two is something to see. One day I hooked a barracuda that looked about 14 inches long. I was horsing him in, as I was after bonefish that day and didn't want to be bothered with any 14-inch cuda. When I had him about halfway in, I saw a silver streak zip through the water and before I knew it, I was dragging in just 7 inches of cuda. The back half had been sheared off as slick as if a knife had been used, and by another cuda that looked, at most, an inch longer than his victim.

Barracuda like a flashy lure and a fast retrieve. Once, while wading Key Largo flats, I saw a good-sized cuda lying motionless straight ahead of me. He was pointing in my direction. I made two casts with a bucktail right to him, but he didn't bat an eye. Then, on my third cast, a puff of wind sent the fly off to the left and I swept it past his nose as fast as I could. He let it pass, then tore after it and struck going away.

"Going away" was right! He hit, came out heading toward the sea, lit about 15 feet beyond where he left the water, bit through my leader, and the last I saw of him he was a mere speck diminishing in the deep water far away.

It is usually difficult to make big cudas hit. They will look at the lure and sometimes swim toward it, but seldom stir themselves to go for it wholeheartedly. When they do, though, it's worth seeing. Popping bugs seem to draw a better response from the larger fish than do the underwater lures. A fast-played popper, with plenty of loud pops, will stir them out of their lethargy now and again, and bring strikes.

The first time I walked along the cliffs of Bermuda, headed for a place to get down to the beach to wade, I saw a school of a dozen barracuda silhouetted against the fine Bermuda sand. I didn't wait to get into the water, but tied a yellow popper to the end of my leader and threw it out in front of them. A fish followed that bug almost to shore before he hit, then came halfway out of the water in his eagerness to have it. He jumped and made the line zip as he sped 20 feet this way and then 20 in the opposite direction, climaxing every spurt with a wild leap. Just as I finally got him to the edge of the cliff, the hook dropped out of his mouth. But as I ran my fingers over the leader tippet, I realized that it was probably just as well, because if I had tried to lift him on that battered tippet, it would have broken.

Perhaps because of the deeper water, the Bermuda barracuda went for yellow poppers better than white and they had a habit of following slowly after it, then easing off a bit, and then going for it hard. They followed lures, it seemed to me, farther than those I have fished for elsewhere.

Probably because of his formidable reputation for snapping lines and stealing lures, not many fly-fishermen go out just for cuda. The Miami Beach Rod and Reel Club and the Sportsmen's Club of Dade County list the sharp-toothed fish in their interclub tournaments, and anglers from those two clubs have turned in some very nice catches. But a great many sportsmen are missing some real fun when they ignore the barracuda.

Barracuda like flashy lures and the silver spoon type of fooler is good medicine to use on them. The OO Huntington Drone, the metalure, and the trix-oreno seem to bring more strikes than do streamers or bucktails. At times cudas will knock the dickens out of poppers and as a rule I prefer to use them, as it is fun to see the fish come tearing up to the surface to hit. Poppers tied on 3/0 Z nickle hooks

180

help, too, in keeping the barracuda's sharp teeth from cutting through the leader.

Spinner-streamer combinations are also strike-bringers, the silver spinner with yellow streamer being the best. All streamers or bucktails used for barracuda should be tied with a silver tinsel body.

And with all types of lures, remember that the faster the retrieve, the better.

14.

Jack Crevalle

 THE jack crevalle is a rough, rugged scrapper and I've often heard fishermen say that they just didn't want to hang into one. That might sound funny to anglers who haven't had dealings with jack, but to those who have it makes sense. When you have done battle with and finally landed one of those flat-bodied gamesters, you want to take a rest. A good long one. They are reckless, hard-hitting *hombres* that don't know what it means to quit. They are not so glamorous and perhaps not so flashy as some of the other salt-water game fish, but for the thrill of a good, old-time, tough fight and the shock of a hard, jolting strike, latch onto a jack.

My first encounter with one was accidental. I was after tarpon, using a big white popping bug because is was cloudy and I couldn't see through the water. Bonnie Smith, who was guiding me, staked out on the edge of a bonefish flat off Islamorada. The water was about 8 feet deep. As I was making a retrieve, I suddenly saw a flash in back of the bug and then had a jolting hit, the fish throwing water high as he took. I struck and watched the line melt from my reel. The fish (I didn't know what it was, then) dashed off 200 feet of line in a jiffy and then swung broadside to the boat and slowed down somewhat. I leaned back on the rod to test his strength. It was plenty. He started to shake his head, rocking the rod tip violently. I could feel the power of him as my hands squeezed the rod butt. It was like holding onto the tail of a bucking bronco. Then he bored for the bottom and I propped the rod butt against my chest and hung on. Then I held it in my right hand for a while because my chest was getting sore. After ten minutes I switched over to my other hand because my right one began to feel as if it might drop off. I kept the pressure on and so did the fish. By this time, Bonnie had told me it was a jack crevalle.

"And," she added, "get ready for a long, long fight."

I was using my Orvis 9½-foot fly rod with the matching GAF line. The leader was tapered down to a 12-pound test tippet. I gave that outfit everything I thought it would take, and that's plenty. Not once during the whole grueling battle did I let up but it was three quarters of an hour after he hit before Bonnie slipped the net under him and brought that jack, still struggling, into the boat. He weighed 8 pounds.

Jack crevalle range from Massachusetts down along the southeastern coast of the United States and throughout the Gulf of Florida. They feed on crabs and smaller fishes in inlets, bays, and channels and on the deeper flats. They are a predaceous fish, and hit their prey fiercely. When you run into a school on the feed, you have all the action you want!

It's something to see a cruising school of jacks working the edge of the mangroves. They go so fast, striking on top as they move along, that an angler is hard put to it to keep ahead of them. Casting to a fast-moving school calls for a fast retrieve. Either streamers or poppers will do the trick, although for such fast fishing, I prefer the streamers. Just toss the fly several feet in front of them and start it back in a hurry. Usually it doesn't get very far before you have a strike, several fish going for it at the same time. These school fish will gobble up almost anything in their path and even the small ones will go for big lures with abandon.

Captain Leo Johnson and I were working the edge of a long narrow flat off Upper Matecumbe Key, one day. The flat was cut through in several places by channels some six feet deep. A tarpon rolled as we approached one of these cuts through the flat and I tossed my big popper where he had been. I didn't even have time for a single pop before a school of jacks appeared from nowhere and one of them hit hard. I started him in and as I watched him use his deep, flat body to fight back with, I marveled at the strength of such a little fish. When he finally came to net, we discovered that he wasn't as big as my hand.

That school of jacks hung around and everytime I would cast to a rolling or cruising tarpon, they would beat the silver king to the lure. I finally took the popper off and put on a fast-sinking streamer and that way managed to get several strikes from tarpon. But before I was through with that fly, the jacks had torn the feathers to pieces.

On another occasion, however, a tarpon turned the tables on a school of jacks to which I was fishing in a hidden lake back in the mangroves off Key Largo. I heard the fish breaking on the surface and saw them nipping along under the mangroves, traveling fast toward me. I waited until they were within range, then dropped the fly in front of them. In a second I was fast to one, and by the time I had landed that one-pound fish, the school was far up the shore line, still breaking and still traveling at the same fast pace.

I picked up the oars and cut across the lake to head them off. Thirty feet in front of the charging fish, I put the fly to them. The rod almost jerked out of my hands and I watched a 10-pound tarpon come out, struggle toward the sky, and throw the hook. He splashed back right into the middle of that school of jacks and they tore the water into little bits getting out of there. That was the last I saw of them.

Jack like brightly colored flies, spinner-streamer combinations, and will hit the spoon-type fly-rod lures almost every time you offer them one. I use the latter lures when I am after the big jacks that lurk in the channels under the coral. I cast to the edge and let the lure sink well down before starting the foot-long jerks so effective with jack. One of the biggest crevalle I ever caught was taken on a #2 silver spinner with a yellow streamer and red hackles. He weighed 10 pounds and took an hour to land.

Long fights with jack are common. Dick Splaine once fought one for three hours and followed the fish in a skiff for over a mile before the fight was over. It hit 15 pounds. Dick was using a light rod and light leader and couldn't put on as much pressure as he wanted, but even with that light tackle, it makes you realize what tough babies those jacks are. I've heard a lot about the "pound for pound" business, but although I am a great admirer

of the smallmouth black bass and love to fish for him—
well, Dr. Henshall certainly called that one wrong.*

The jack is a wild-hitting package of dynamite that
will strike at almost any lure you choose to offer. Size,
color, and type make little difference. But for fishing the
channels where the big fish work, it seems more fun to me
to fish for them with a popping bug, either yellow or
white, or a combination of red and white, and yellow and
white. The jack will hit poppers viciously and often, but
when you run into a school of the fish, the streamer works
better and as long as you can keep up to the school, you
can get a strike out of almost every cast. Streamers with
a red hackle and yellow feathers, and those with red
hackle and white feathers stand out. And since the 3/0
hook seems to work better than the 1/0 on the bigger
jack, I nearly always use the streamer or popper on
the larger hook.

* "Inch for inch and pound for pound, the gamest fish that swims."
J. A. Henshall in *The Book of the Black Bass.*

15.

Deep-Water Fly-Fishing

SCHOOL FISH

Fishing a fly in deep water is a long cry from the use for which the fly rod was originally designed. But there is plenty of fly fishing sport to be found in deep water and many of the salt water game fish that will surface and hit small lures are ideal light tackle game. School fish of many species range over thousands of miles and their yen for streamers and bucktails and poppers can furnish sport for anglers on both coasts of the United States. And although school fish are unpredictable in many ways, it is possible, when conditions are just right, to have mighty good fishing from schools of spotted sea trout, sea trout, dolphin, mackerel, stripers, bluefish, jack crevalle, and in some places, bonito.

In the Gulf Stream, where the colorful dolphin dwell, a cast of a streamer to almost any bit of floating matter will meet with a slashing reception from the beautiful game-ster. Old planks, boards, floating masses of grass—all at times shelter dolphin and when you run into a school of them, they will hit the fly at practically every cast. Dolphin are just about as fast as any fish that swims, as strong as Jersey bulls, and their jumps are spectacular to the

189

nth degree. After a certain amount of fishing, they grow scared, dive deep, and that is that, but while they do stay around you can have sport that is out of this world. And sometimes, if you feel that they are becoming suspicious of your offering, you can tie on a new lure and bring renewed strikes.

Another trick known to most anglers who have taken dolphin is to hook a fish and then tie the line to the stern of the boat. The school will follow that fish for a long time, and give you lots of chances to cast to them as they do so.

Two years ago, Lee Cuddy of Miami landed sixteen dolphin in one afternoon, in the Gulf Stream. He took them all on fly rod and streamer, from a single school. They ran from 2 to 5 pounds apiece, so you can imagine the sport Lee had with those brilliant-colored speedsters.

You never know when you are going to get into some school fishing, either. One day I was fishing alone, bass bugging on Seneca Creek on the Chesapeake. As I was not very far from the mouth of the river, I occasionally glanced toward the bay, where at that time of year, schools of stripers often worked. Soon I saw gulls diving and wheeling quite near the shore. I cranked up the motor and started for the scene of action. As I steamed along, I saw more gulls coming from all directions, and also counted twelve boats of various designs, from skiffs to charter boats, bearing down on the busy birds.

Pretty soon I saw the feeding fish break water, and when I was within casting distance, I hove to and started to throw to them. They were small fish, running around 20 inches, but I took three in very quick succession. Then

190

boats crowded in from all sides, trolling through and around the school, the fish dove, and I started my motor and went putt-putting back to my bass bugging.

In the deep water of bays and sounds, school fish can often be found feeding on the surface. Most of them will stay around long enough to allow you a bit of fishing before they go down. Then you search for new schools, or try to locate the same one when it comes to the top again. For that kind of fishing you have a scout in the form of the gulls, which always keep on the lookout for feeding fish. When they sight a school, they dash madly toward them from all directions, to feed on the cut-up pieces of bait fish that the larger fish have slashed through.

Recently, with Warry Gillet of Baltimore, I went out from Tilgham's, on the eastern shore of the Chesapeake Bay. We had only been out a short time when we saw the gulls about a quarter of a mile away. The captain speeded up the boat and as we neared the diving birds, we spotted fish breaking on the surface. As soon as we were within casting range, we began to throw small white bucktails into the edge of the school. I had three strikes on my first retrieve and finally, on the fourth hit, hooked the fish. It was a blue that weighed about a pound and he did a lot of high-class fighting before I boated him. Blues are fast and it was fun to watch them slashing at our lures.

We stayed with that school for twenty minutes, the captain holding the boat off while we cast to them. I don't remember how many we landed, as we put most of them back. Of the six we kept to eat, three looked like better than 3 pounds.

Salt Water Fly Fishing

When that school finally sounded, we cruised slowly along scanning the sky for the telltale gathering of gulls, and watching the surface of the water for breaking fish. An hour later we again struck paydirt, this time a school of stripers that went from 3 to 5 pounds. We did a land-office business with them, too. They were on the prod and hit both white and yellow popping bugs and when we switched to white bucktails, they hit that lure just as hard.

And that is typical of school fishing of most kinds—once you find the school, fishing is good!

Along Bermuda's famous pink beaches, in the summer of 1949, I had several days of unexcelled school fishing of a kind that was entirely new to me, and which has become increasingly popular with both Bermudians and visitors to the island, since that time. From the picturesque sandstone cliffs above the beach, Louis Mowbray pointed out a swift moving pepper of dots in the clear water below.

"Pompano," he said.

"Lots of them," agreed Pete Perinchief. "Let's go!" And in a few minutes the six of us—Jimmie Williams, Wilfred Higgs, and Pete Perinchief, all of the Bermuda News Bureau, Louis Mowbray, curator of the aquarium at Flatts, Brose Gosling, well known Bermuda angler, and I—were clambering down the rugged shore to the beach.

The flashy gaff topsail pompano, called by scientists *trachinotus Palometa*, is a little bit of a fellow as salt-water game fish go. His top weight is around 4 pounds. But on light tackle he is a handful of hard-charging, hard-fighting fun. The ideal way to fish for him is to don a pair of swimming trunks and either stand on the sand or wade out into the surf. The fish swim parallel to the shore line, darting in

192

now and then, after the break of the surf, and snatching titbits of small crabs and other crustaceans out of the swirl of the undertow. They remind me of sanderlings, those tiny shore birds one sees running up and down the beaches, always just in back of or in advance of the rise and fall of the waves. Standing on the beach, you can sometimes see the pompano in the curl of the breakers, the long streamers of their caudal fins waving like pennants, to herald the tough, racy, broken field runner of the crashing surf.

Louis landed the first fish that day, and then, lined up abreast, we were all fishing and soon all had strikes. First our line stood knee-deep in the water, then waist deep, and soon we were beyond the curl of the breakers as the fish were scared out of the shallows. Finally I looked down the line and was convulsed to discover a bodyless head, apparently floating on the water and accompanied only by a pair of rod-wielding arms—all that could be seen of Pete as he pursued the last bevy of pompano flitting seaward.

Pompano will hit a small white streamer with a thump, but the flash, shine and enticing action of the OO Huntington Drone causes them to really discard caution and go for it with a rush. Either type of lure will take pompano, however, as will a white streamer, silver-spinner combination.

Angling for pompano does not require long casts. Throws of 20 to 30 feet will catch them, but the bigger fish seem to lie further out and casts of 40 to 50 feet will bring in more 2- and 3-pounders. Those larger fish will give a battle far in excess of expectations. Their deep, compact bodies make for a rousing fight and their constant contact with the surf makes them very strong. A 2-pound fish will take your casting line and 100 feet of backing in a jiffy and before you have beached your catch you will be ready to bow to him as a formidable, rough-and-tumble scrapper.

In the phenomenally clear Bermuda water you can see the pompano come for the lure and see him hit it. Sometimes you can watch a whole school zipp through the breakers, the black dorsal, anal, and caudal fins waving like the standards of a troop of cavalrymen. That kind of fishing is fun—fun breasting the surf, watching the waves so that an extra large one doesn't roll you over; fun, too, jumping up to ride the big swells, then making the cast and waiting for the hit. It's a different kind of fishing for one of the tastiest fish that ever tickled a palate and for a swell little gamester who lives amid surroundings of enchantment.

CHUMMING

Nearly everyone has seen the chumming method, used at some time or another, to bring fish up from the depths. Food is thrown on the surface of the water and as it drifts away with the tide, fish smell or see it and come to it to feed. This brings them within reach of light tackle and allows the angler to offer them an artificial lure with a fair chance of it being seen. It is old stuff, and has been practiced for many years up and down the Atlantic Coast, but generally for bait fishermen. The greatest drawback for the fly rodder is that, due to the cost of a charter boat, he usually winds up with two or three other anglers

194

who use heavier tackle. When unable to land his fish quickly, the man with the fly outfit is subjected to scowls, leers, and many mutterings as well as a few good, hearty cuss words from those who want their fish in fast.

But on occasion, the light rod and artificial lure has accounted for more than its share of the fish that come up the chum line. On a trip he made out of Southport, L. I., in 1935, with chummers, Dick Splaine used his fly rod to account for thirty-five of sixty-nine sea trout landed that day, among four anglers. Of course, he admits considerable interference with the bait anglers' lines, as every time he got a fish on, they had to scramble to get their lines in or become tangled. While Dick used streamers for some of the fish, he found the fly rod tin liz by far the most potent lure.

The chum material used varies according to locale. On the Atlantic Coast, where stripers and sea trout are the swimmers most sought for, shrimp is used. At present prices, it is rather an expensive chum but it does bring the fish up when the water has seemed devoid of them.

Some anglers simply cut up larger fish into little pieces for chum, while in Bermuda every two-year-old child can lisp to you that "Bermuda fish like fry." These small minnows, called "hogmouthed fry" are caught in a cast net, placed in a bucket, and carried to the deep-water fishing grounds. Anchovies and pilchards are used, too, but they sink a little too quickly to serve as a good chum for fly fishing. In Bermuda the water is too deep for most fly-rod angling and even right along the shore line or over the reefs, the fish just won't come up through that much water to a surface offering of an artificial lure. The only answer is to chum.

Over there, you chum in water from 5 feet to 10 fathoms deep and you never know what will come up from the bottom. Some of the fish which appear are capable of tearing off great lengths of line from your reel, and some of them are experts at diving to cut the leader on under-water growths. But there are quite a few that are fun to catch and are sure bets almost every time you go out. The yellowtail, bonito, and amberjack will show, first breaking far off, and gradually moving up the chum line to within casting distance. Though all of them hit best if the lure is floating dead along with the chum, the bonito and amberjack will occasionally take a moving lure. Yellowtail will do so only when they are in a school that is traveling. And all of them, with the possible exception of bonito, like the fly to match the fry very closely.

Bonito are hard-hitting, hard-fighting fish, and usually only appear in small numbers. Seldom have I seen more than five or six at one time in the chum line. They seem to hang on the outskirts of the other fish, but when they make up their minds to take, they go for the fly like a flash. The bonito will hit almost any type of streamer and even likes the small fly-rod sized silver spoons.

Very few amberjack are taken on fly rods, but they are there, and the hope always hovers in the angler's mind that he will tie into a 20- or 25-pounder. When all the fish feeding in his chum line suddenly take off, he peers down into the depths searching eagerly for the big, dim shape, which means an amberjack. They don't take often, but when they do, action is fast and furious.

196

To me, the mangrove or gray snapper is one of the most interesting and exasperating fish in Bermuda waters. They are everywhere—under coral heads, over submerged reefs, off wharfs, under moored boats, around bridges, and even just beyond the surf. The average snapper in the ocean weighs between 4 and 7 pounds, while in the bays and sounds they go as high as 16. And they are just about the smartest fish I have encountered anywhere. Well dubbed "the sea lawyer," the snapper is a wily fellow that knows his way around and will not be fooled by anything but the most accurate fly reproduction of fry. They are so smart that more than once I have had the inclination to feed them buckshot rather than flies.

One day Louis Mowbray took me out to the reefs after snapper. We had some small white bucktails which I thought matched the fry very well. We anchored, tossed a few handsful of the fry overboard, and got ready. Immediately several big gray shapes drifted up from the bottom and began to cut through the fry, breaking the surface as they fed. I tossed my fly out and started retrieving it. Several snappers moved politely aside to let it pass.

"Don't retrieve it," said Louis. "Let it float still, like the fry."

I tried that. The fly floated along nicely with the fry. A big snapper dashed for it, then for no apparent reason put on the brakes, hesitated and wheeled away. I let the fly drift. Another one made for it and this time, thinking he had it, I struck. That one wasn't there, either. So I tapered my leader down from 8- to 4-pound test and put on another fly that looked even more like the fry. This time

I did business, all right, but the snapper dove and cut the leader on something sharp on the bottom.

As we continued to throw chum over, the fish grew wilder and wilder, cutting through it, gobbling it up, and coming closer to the boat all the time.

"Look!" cried Louis. "I wanted you to see this. Watch that black line running back from their eyes. The harder they feed, the blacker it gets. That's when you can expect a hit—they get so excited with all that food around that they become careless."

Things worked out just as he had said. As we tried each new spot, I would hold my casting while the snappers came up and began to feed, and then when that stripe was good and black I would put the lure out there and get immediate action.

When you hook a snapper that weighs more than 10 pounds, things happen in a hurry. They are tough *hombres,* with sharp teeth and a full bag of tricks. I had four on in one afternoon, all of them estimated at better than 10 pounds, and each of them departed with my fly. In fact, those four linger in my memory as the "fearsome four." They live (and I purposely use the present tense) in the channel right under the Aquarium Bridge at Flatts, Bermuda. It's a place that every Bermuda angler knows and has been fished so heavily that those snappers can tell you the name of every lure in a sporting-goods showcase. They've tasted quite a few, and in fact probably have a nice collection of lures cached away under the coral. But they are as tricky as wolverines, and no one has yet pulled one of the quartet out.

I hooked all four, as I said, and two of them whipped

off 200 feet of backing, before cutting my leader. The third dove straight down and cut me off before I knew what was going on. And the fourth got me into a fight that drew a crowd. He had me under the bridge, where I had to slink along a foot-wide strip of slippery concrete, and over the bridge, where I had to scramble between a dozen little British autos and a couple of horse carriages. And finally, when he got tired of that, he slipped the leader around the sharp edge of the bridge abutment and cut it off as neatly as you please. When the line went slack, I heard a gentle "aaah!" from above, as the whole crowd let their breath out in a single sigh. And then the traffic moved on.

I hooked those fish again, too, and again. But they were always too strong, and I couldn't hold them long enough to tire them. They just cut the leader and went away from there.

In Bermuda some chumming is done along the beaches, too. It is not unusual to see anglers tearing down the shore, clad in bathing suits and carrying a loaf of bread under one arm and a rod under the other. They break the bread into little pieces, wade out just beyond the curl of the breakers, and toss the crumbs on the water. Soon you see the dark dorsal and anal fins of the game little palometa pompano as he flits through the water, feeding on the bread crumbs.

On the one trip to Bermuda, I landed an even dozen species that are not generally regarded as fly-rod fish by the expedient of using chum. These included amberjack, Bermuda bonito, Bermuda chub, yellowtail, gwelly (crevalle), horse-eye amberjack, gray or mangrove snapper, bonefish, barracuda, sennet (small barracuda), mackerel and pompano. And, of course, there are many other potential fly takers in these and other deeper waters, to be coaxed up from the depths for the sport of those anglers, like myself, to whom the fly rod offers the ultimate in sport.